LOOKING Guud
NATURALLY

LOOKING GOOD
NATURALLY

JILL NICE

UNWIN HYMAN

First published in Great Britain in 1986 by
Unwin Hyman Publishers
Denmark House
37/39 Queen Elizabeth Street
London SE1 2QB

ISBN 0 7135 2741 2

Typeset by Wordsmiths, Street, Somerset
Printed and originated in Singapore

This book was designed and produced by The Paul Press Ltd, 22,
Bruton Street, London W1X 7DA

Art Editor	Tony Paine
Project Editor	Emma Warlow
Art Assistant	Sarah McDonald
Illustrations	Christine Berrington at Garden Studios
Still Life Photography	Andrew Hayward
Picture Researcher	Liz Eddison
Art Director	Stephen McCurdy
Managing Editor	Elizabeth Longley
Editorial Director	Jeremy Harwood
Managing Director	Nigel Perryman

CONTENTS

FOREWORD

When I was a beauty therapist, I often found that women regarded the care of their skin, hair, hands, feet and figure as a necessary, but unexciting, chore. Part of the incentive to produce this book sprang from my belief that personal beauty care can and should be enjoyable. Being able to make your own cosmetics adds a new dimension to your beauty routine – you can feel proud of your creative achievements, as well as in the spectacular effects they have on your appearance. It is really satisfying to know that you can make the most of yourself simply by following a basic beauty regime and using your own home-made cosmetics.

The recipes and remedies in this book follow, by and large, the traditional methods that have been passed down through the generations. The powers of herbs, on which so many of these old recipes relied, are as potent as they ever were and modern women can learn just how to harness those effective powers in treatments for every part of their body. Most of the other ingredients used are also traditional, though nowadays, of course, we are rather more cautious about using certain substances in home-made preparations than were our predecessors. Animal-derivatives, such as spermacetti wax and turtle oil, for instance, were the staple ingredients of many cosmetic products in the last century; and we know which natural ingredients, such as belladonna and certain mineral salts, can be dangerous. It is very important to feel happy and safe with the products we use on our skin and hair, which is another of my reasons for encouraging people to make their own selection. You know exactly what the contents of each preparation are, and need have no qualms about allergic reactions or suspect ingredients as you might if you were using commercial cosmetics.

Combining the best of the old with the best of the new is the secret to a contented lifestyle. Modern dietetic and dermatological knowledge confirms the importance of pure, natural substances for health and beauty – an assurance, if one were needed, that our ancestors had the right ideas when it came to creating cosmetic preparations. In this book, I have tried to provide a wide variety of both unusual and basic recipes, so that you can experiment to find the ideal range of products to suit your needs. I hope that, having explored the contents of the book, you will be encouraged to discover for yourself just how much fun caring for yourself the natural way can be.

JILL NICE

CHAPTER ONE

NATURE'S WAY

For centuries natural and organic substances have been used in beauty preparations. These recipes, tried and tested by generations of women, have been handed down through the years and are as effective now as they were then.

Following the traditional examples, today's woman can enjoy making herself more beautiful the natural way, in the confidence that modern research has endorsed the beliefs of ancient civilizations regarding the curative properties of many natural ingredients. The vitamins, proteins and minerals found in fresh fruits and vegetables, cereals, yeasts, yoghurt, honey and eggs, and the healing powers of herbs can do nothing but good when combined to care for your skin, body and hair. The basic principles of natural beauty therapy form the foundation of this book — once you have learnt them, you can enjoy putting theory into practice when you create your own cosmetics.

Nature's Way

Women are becoming increasingly aware that natural and organic substances can be used effectively in the care of their skin, body and hair. Natural equivalents of commercial cosmetic products are easily prepared at home, once the basic techniques of natural beautification are understood.

Of course, natural beauty is not skin deep and it takes more than high quality cosmetics to promote the radiance we associate with healthy good looks. A wholesome diet, plenty of fresh air, exercise and sleep form the foundations of an efficient beauty routine, which is reinforced by a carefully researched personal care programme.

The natural beauty tradition

Long before Cleopatra bathed in asses' milk, discerning women of ancient civilizations realized that fermented milk cured infections, that honey nourished and gave energy and that sun-ripened grain, seeds and fruits could provide health-giving oils. They saw quite clearly that what was beneficial to the body also appeared to benefit the skin..

Unhappily, these beliefs, though tried and tested over the centuries, have not always been adhered to. In the early 18th century, for instance, there was a dangerous vogue among the fashion-conscious élite for employing such crude poisonous cosmetic aids as ground alabaster to whiten the skin, coloured lead to paint the eyelids and deadly belladonna to brighten the eyes. However, fashions soon changed and as the century came to a end, many women tended to use only those products made from pure ingredients readily to hand in kitchen and garden.

These natural recipes, passed down from generation to generation, are a discreet but integral part of many Victorian manuals for the gentlewoman. Cucumber to cool, lettuce for sunburn, elderflower milk for freckles and attar of roses to perfume bathing water are just some of the staples that were described. From the secret diaries of great beauties came descriptions of roast figs pulverized with honey to soften the hands, powdered roots and oils for the hair and unguents, spiced with essence of jasmine and bergamot, to tone the body.

So much for tradition and legend. Now, what about the facts? It has been scientifically proven that raw fruit and vegetables contain an abundance of vitamins, minerals, proteins and oils. A raw food diet invigorates your entire system and brings your body the resources necessary for skin and hair that gleam with health. These foods can also be used in external beauty treatments, either applied in their natural state or combined with other natural ingredients,

The glow of healthy beauty has been admired by men and prized by women throughout the ages. Beauty secrets relying on purely natural ingredients are as effective today as they have ever been and are just as easily employed.

such as perfumed oils or herbal infusions, to pamper and care for skin and hair – in the most natural way.

Individual preparations

Whether or not you believe that commercial cosmetics are harmful, it is certain that natural ingredients can do nothing but good. Preparing your own natural cosmetics has the added advantage of catering for entirely personal tastes and requirements. You can make as much or as little as you wish of any preparation, choose the ingredients which are readily available and attractive to you and enjoy the creative satisfaction of producing an individual range of beauty products.

Another great advantage of preparing your own cosmetics and learning about the curative potential of natural ingredients is that you can plan for the varying needs of your skin. Essential day-to-day creams and lotions are the basis of your beauty routine, but once you know your skin's peculiarities, you can supplement them with the appropriate remedies *(see pp48-51)*. A tired face, an attack of itching, an outbreak of pimples, sunburn or an incipient cold sore, can all be relieved quickly with a little expertise.

Producing your own beauty aids also means that you can be sure that there are no harmful chemical or potentially allergenic natural ingredients in your preparations. By making thorough skin reaction tests *(see p27)*, you can learn which ingredients to avoid and will suffer no unexpected or unpleasant side-effects from the recipes you choose. Worrying minor skin infections, blackheads and a sunburnt nose can all be healed with the use of specific and carefully selected herbs. It must be stressed, however, that for any prolonged or serious skin infection you should seek professional advice.

Some golden rules

When you start to prepare your own cosmetics, it is vital that everything you use – ingredients, utensils and containers – is scrupulously clean. Ideally, storage jars should be dark or opaque to prevent direct light reaching the contents and causing deterioration or discoloration. To ensure that they are sterile, wash the jars in warm soapy water. Rinse them well and place them upside down in a warm oven to dry. Be careful not to leave them in too long in case they crack.

Once you are sure that everything you are using is clean and fresh, you can feel confident that your cosmetics will be absolutely pure and of the highest quality. Having made cleanliness your first priority, your next concern must be to

Nature's way

ensure that the products you make are stored sensibly. Where necessary, the recipes in this book specify how each preparation should be stored, and for how long, but as a general rule when working with perishable ingredients remember the maxim 'If you can eat it do not keep it'. On the other hand, commercially produced ingredients, such as oils, resins, creams and powders, have a relatively long shelf life if stored correctly in dark, dry, well-sealed containers.

Obviously, home-made cosmetics, like their commercial counterparts, will not keep indefinitely, so be wary of preparations if you know they have been around for some time. A little care and thought will suffice to ensure that your own cosmetics are pure and safe to use.

Self-indulgence does pay

It does not matter how naturally excellent your cosmetics are if you neglect your general health. The condition of your skin, hair, teeth and nails is dictated by the condition of your body, so take care of your inner as well as your outer self. Plenty of fresh air, exercise – swimming and walking are the best – enough sleep, a healthy diet, less alcohol, fewer cigarettes and the consumption of unlimited amounts of fresh, sparkling water to eliminate toxins are the secrets of enduring beauty. Once you get into the rhythm of a healthy lifestyle you will find that the way you feel and look as a result encourages you to sustain it. Incorporate the exercises and diet which afford you maximum exhilaration, enjoyment and energy into your daily routine to guarantee a glowing beauty from within.

There is nothing decadent about spending time on the care of your face and body. It is an absolute necessity and you owe it to yourself to feel good from top to toe. Bath or shower every day, making sure that you have a relaxing massage afterwards with one of your special body lotions, paying particular attention to your legs, upper shoulders and back *(see p100-101)*. Enjoy massaging your face *(see pp38-41)* and watching the positive results of a thoughtful beauty routine. Look after your hands and feet *(see pp80-1)*. Keep your hair in good condition by using naturally mild shampoos, conditioners and rinses *(see pp62-73)* and having it trimmed regularly.

You have only one body. If you take good care of it from within by eating the proper food, taking regular exercise and paying attention to its appearance, it will do you credit. Above all, remember that your face reflects your personality. Good nature, good humour and a zest for life make some of the greatest contributions to natural beauty.

Healthy eating encourages beautiful skin, hair, eyes, teeth and nails, so it is vitally important to establish a well-balanced nutritious diet if you want to pave the way for long-lasting natural beauty.

NATURAL INGREDIENTS

Apart from fruit and vegetables, the following ingredients are either readily available or can be ordered from most chemists, health and wholefood shops.

Alcohol Many cleansers and toners contain alcohol; this has astringent qualities and removes grease and excess oil. It also acts as a preservative and is necessary to lift and diffuse essential oils in colognes and perfumes. Vodka is the best alternative to pure ethyl alcohol.

Almond The oil obtained from almonds is rich and pure. It is used extensively in beauty preparations. A white milk used in cleansers and astringents is obtained by soaking ground almonds in milk or water. Gently abrasive facial and body scrubs sometimes contain ground almonds and oatmeal.

Alum A fine, white mineral powder. Soluble and astringent, it is used in skin lotions.

Apricot Apricots contain a fine and highly nourishing oil, rich in Vitamin A, which improves the condition and elasticity of the skin, guarding against the appearance of severe stretch marks and smoothing wrinkles. The pulp of both fresh and dried fruit is used in face masks. The finely ground shell and kernel of the stone are used in facial and body scrubs.

Arrowroot A thickening agent, like cornflour and laundry starch, used in face packs and bath preparations.

Avocado The oil of avocado is rich in Vitamins A and B, minerals and lecithin and is of value as a moisturizer, particularly in hot climates.

Beeswax The yellow wax found in natural honeycombs. It is a nourishing emollient with a high melting point. When mixed with borax *(see below)* it becomes an emulsifier (ie. prevents the separation of water and oils combined in a recipe).

Benzoin (or **Gum Benjamin**, or **Friars Balsam**) An aromatic resin which is valuable for its antiseptic and preservative properties. Tincture of benzoin is frequently added to tonics, toners and moisturizers.

Borax A slightly antiseptic, acid powder used primarily as an emulsifier. It has detergent properties and is therefore useful in making soap and shampoo.

Bran A frequently used substitute for soap. It is also used in facial and body scrubs and instant cleansers.

Brewer's yeast A fine powder rich in Vitamin B, minerals and proteins which is used in cleansing masks for oily skins.

Buttermilk A sweetish whey produced in butter-making that contains calcium, proteins and some vitamins. Cleansing and bleaching effectively, it also tightens enlarged pores, soothes, cools and is an excellent sunburn lotion.

Camphor This can be obtained as oil, spirits or crystals. It has a healing and tightening effect and is valuable in masks and toners for its astringent and stimulant qualities.

Carrots The raw grated vegetable and extracted juices make excellent quick cleansers, masks, tonics and nourishing skin foods for problem skins, particularly those which are dry, irritated or sunburnt. Carrots are a rich source of Vitamin A which promotes healing and counteracts infection. Carrot oil is frequently used in anti-wrinkle creams.

Castor oil This is obtained from the seeds of the castor oil plant. It is smooth, rich and mainly used in hair conditioners, massage oils, lip salves and soap. Turkey Red is a variety of castor oil used in bath oils.

Cocoa butter A rich, expensive wax obtained from the cocoa bean which makes good quality nourishing creams for ageing skins, or those suffering from the effects of sun, wind or excessive dryness. It is also used extensively in hair conditioners, moisturizers, cleansers and hand creams.

Coconut oil The oil obtained from the flesh of the coconut is fine and rich. It sets solid but melts as soon as it is warmed, which makes it perfect as an instant suntan lotion. Used in conditioners, moisturizing creams, lip salves and bath oils.

Cream Cream can be used as a nourishing base for face masks and makes an excellent massage lotion with or without the addition of other ingredients.

Cucumber The cool green juice and flesh of the cucumber is used extensively in cosmetics. Soothing, healing, and slightly astringent; it is used in masks, cleansers and toners for sallow and oily skins with enlarged pores. It can also be used to soothe sunburn and tired eyes.

Eggs Eggs are packed full of protein, iron, lecithin and vitamins. They are cheap, nourishing and versatile. Egg whites are astringent and can be used as face masks for oily or blemished skins. Yolks are used for enriching face masks. The whole egg is used in hair conditioners and bath oils.

Emulsifying wax A commercial product, necessary to bind oil and water together into a cream.

Fuller's earth A fine grey powder rich in minerals which is mixed with other ingredients to make highly absorbent and cleansing face masks. Occasionally used in "dry" shampoo.

Gelatine A natural animal glue that is soluble and used in setting lotions and nail creams.

Glycerine A thick colourless liquid that can be dissolved in water. Because it is oily, it is often added to cleansers and toners for dry skins. It is also used in bath oils and hand lotions.

Gum arabic and Gum Tragacanth These are natural soluble resins used to thicken and stabilize creams and lotions.

Honey Honey is a natural healer, extensively used in skin preparations. Rich in minerals and vitamins, it is a unique skin food with soothing therapeutic properties. It is also used as a binding agent.

Kaolin A fine white powder with unique "drawing" qualities. It is used as a binding agent in face masks and in of preparations for hands and hair.

Lanolin A rich sticky fat extracted from sheep's wool. There are two types of purified lanolin – anhydrous and hydrous. Lanolin is easily absorbed by the skin and is both nourishing and moisturizing. It is commonly used in the preparation of cosmetic creams.

Lecithin A nutritious emulsifying substance, found for instance in soya beans and egg yolk, which is commercially available in the form of a soft beige powder. It contains phosphorous and protein and is used mainly in enriching creams and face masks. As a food supplement, it is very effective in the treatment of acne.

Lemon Lemons contain citric acid and Vitamin C. Lemon juice restores the natural acid balance of the skin, counteracts infection and acts as a bleach. Together with the finely ground rind and lemon oil, it is used in an astringent range of preparations, from face toners for problem skins to hair rinses.

Milk Milk, both fresh and soured, acts as an effective cleanser to nourish and soften the skin. Dried milk is used to thicken face masks.

Myrrh An antiseptic and preservative resin sold as a tincture and added to cosmetics to prolong their life. It is also used as a remedy for mild mouth infections and in some perfumes.

Oats Oats are rich in protein and minerals. Finely ground into oatmeal, they are frequently used as as alternative to soap, oatmeal is an excellent base for face masks, scrubs, and soaps.

Olive oil A rich, but rather pungent oil. Its heavy smell limits its uses in cosmetics, but it makes an excellent hair conditioner and tanning oil.

Oranges Oranges contain large amounts of Vitamins A and C which makes the juice a zesty addition to skin tonics and masks. Orange oil and orange flower water are used in colognes and add fragrance to all beauty preparations. The finely ground peel is a useful abrasive ingredient for masks, scrubs and tooth powders. Bergamot oil and oil of neroli are commercially obtained from the Bergamot orange.

Peach The pulp of the fresh peach is used in face masks, cleansers and moisturizers for dry skins. Peach nut oil is fragrant, enriching and is used in nourishing face creams and hair conditioners.

Pumpkin The oil extracted from pumpkin seeds is very healing, especially for sunburnt or wind dried skin.

Safflower and sunflower oils These are both obtained from plants and are rich in polyunsaturates. They are pure and fine, and cheap enough to use freely in beauty preparations.

Sea salt This is used as a slightly antiseptic and abrasive body scrub for rough and hard skin. It is a natural tooth powder.

Soap Castile and olive oil soap is absolutely pure. Grated, it is used in shampoos, bubble baths and soap making.

Sulphur A yellow mineral powder used to heal acne. It can cause an allergic reaction.

Tea Tea contains tannin which absorbs ultraviolet rays. Tea has soothing and healing properties and will alleviate the sting of sunburn. Use tea bag compresses to soothe tired eyes.

Vinegar Herbal and cider vinegars have remedial properties and are used in hair rinses and conditioners. Added to washing and bath water, vinegar cleanses, softens, restores lost acidity to the skin and reduces itchiness caused by minor allergies. The correct proportions to use in the bath are 8 parts water to 1 part vinegar.

Water Since there is a high percentage of water in creams and lotions, it is absolutely essential that only bottled, purified or boiled water is used to avoid contamination.

Wheatgerm Rich in vitamins and minerals, wheatgerm is exceptionally beneficial in face masks and body scrubs. It also improves the condition of the skin generally. Wheatgerm oil is rich in Vitamin E and has extraordinary healing properties.

White wax Paraffin wax is a plain odourless wax used as an economical alternative to beeswax.

Witch hazel An astringent, antiseptic distillation of the bark of *hamamelis virginiana* used widely in pharmaceutical preparations and cosmetics.

Yoghurt Milk turns to yoghurt when curdled by specific bacteria. Yoghurt contains bacteria-destroying enzymes and has a beneficial effect when used in the treatment of problem skins. It is a highly effective beauty aid and is used in face washes, body and facial scrubs and hair conditioners.

Zinc oxide A white powder with antiseptic, astringent properties. It is used as a dusting powder and in soothing lotions.

HERBAL HELPERS/1

At one time, herbs were the only form of medicinal therapy available to mankind; they were used in every aspect of physical treatment from midwifery to beautification. In general terms they deserve their magic reputation, for by some strange symbiotic evolution they seem to grow just where man needs them the most. By incorporating them in your beauty preparations, you will see for yourself that healing herbs really *do* work as treatments for all manner of cosmetic problems, from blemished skin to falling hair.

How to use herbs
Fresh and dried herbs can be used in many ways. A selection of suitable herbs can be simmered, mashed and applied as a simple face pack, or used in a basic facial "steamer" *(see pp36-7)*. They can be finely chopped and added to face masks and nourishing creams, but the most popular method of mixing these valuable ingredients into beauty preparations is by incorporating an infusion *(see p20)* or decoction *(see p20)* of the chosen herbs into the recipe.

The essential oils of herbs and some plants are added to cosmetics chiefly for their fragrance, but some, such as rose, geranium and lavender, have strong therapeutic qualities, particularly when used to treat ageing skin. They are the result of a complex, concentrated distillation process. They are expensive but well worth buying.

Herbal oils *(see p21)*, which are very economical to make and therefore can be used more lavishly, are the result of softening herbs and flowers by soaking them in oil and leaving them in full sunlight. This is a process easily achieved at home *(see p21)*. Although these oils do not have the lasting fragrance of essential oils, they are excellent for

massaging the skin of the face and body, particularly in the cases of sunburn or windburn and dehydration. This maceration technique is also used to make herbal vinegars and tinctures using wine, vinegar, alcohol and surgical spirits *(see p21)*.

Essential oils and tinctures have a relatively long shelf life. Herbal oils and vinegars will keep for at least six months in first-class condition, but infusions and decoctions must be stored in a refrigerator and kept for no longer than three days.

If you have neither the time nor the space to cultivate a herb garden in your garden, then I advocate growing a few herbs on the windowsill in your kitchen or bathroom *(see p18)*. Easily-cultivated herbs like mint, parsley, thyme, sage, chervil, fennel, rosemary and the brightly coloured pot marigold and geranium (pelargonium) will thrive in these conditions, thus benefiting your health, beauty and cooking.

Where to buy and how to store your herbal compounds

Essential oils, unusual herbs and tinctures can be bought at specialist herbalists. Loose dried herbs can be bought at health and wholefood shops. Store just enough dried herbs to suit your needs, but keep them, like oils and tinctures, in opaque jars or boxes, tightly sealed and away from direct light. Keep all such containers labelled with contents and the date of purchase.

Herbal helpers/2

GROWING INDOOR HERBS

- You can stand small flowerpots of individual herbs on a tray just inside your window. Water them from the bottom and give them a quarter turn each day to ensure that the light reaches every side.

- The herbs which grow best indoors are chervil, margoram, golden sage,camomile, hyssop, lady's mantle, lavender and dill.
Grow mint and lemon balm separately, because their roots will spread and choke other plants.

- Parsley, "prostrate" rosemary, thyme and basil can be grown in hanging baskets in the window.

- Terracotta crocus pots, each hole filled with a different herb are an elegant and efficient way to grow herbs on your windowsill.

Camomile	Use the flowers to make gently astringent infusion for cleansers, conditioners and hair rinses, and herbal oils. Has soothing, cooling properties.
Chervil	Use the leaves to make astringent infusions, or extract their juice. Added to cleansers and conditioners to treat ageing skin.
Cleavers or Goosegrass	Use the whole dried herb to make sweet, mildly astringent infusions. Added to cleansers and tonic for climatically damaged skin. Has deodorizing properties.
Comfrey	Use the root to make decoctions, the leaves to ma infusions. Has antiseptic healing properties when added to creams, lotions and steamers.
Cornflower	Use the blue flowers to make infusions for tonic fresheners and cleansers. Also used in soothing eyewashes.
Dandelion	Use the flowers to make healing infusions or decoctions for cleansers, face packs and steame Use the sap from the stem in bleaching, healing creams for freckles, warts and blemishes.
Elderflower	Use the flowers to make mildly bleaching infusion for softening cleansers, toners and conditioners. Use the leaves to make healing decoctions for blemished, sunburnt or windburnt skin.
Eucalyptus	Use the leaves to make antiseptic, invigorating decoctions for skin care products and baths. Hea skin eruptions and sunburn. Destroys mouth odou
Fennel	Use the chopped leaves to make soothing, stimulating infusions for masks, cleansers, toners and steamers for ageing skin. Destroys mouth odour.
Garlic and onion	Use the juice in antiseptic and smoothing creams and cleansers for ageing skin.
Geranium	Use the flowers and leaves softened in water, or essential oil to add to healing and rejuvenating cleansers and creams for oily and ageing skin.
Houseleek	Crush the leaves and use them to make healing creams and ointments.
Hyssop	Use the leaves and flowering tips to make healing infusions to treat acne. The oil is used in creams a body rubs to relieve aches and pains.
Lady's mantle	Use the juice from the leaves as a tonic for oily sk or added to creams for dry skin. Has healing and bleaching properties and soothes inflamed skin.

vender Use the leaves and flowers to make antiseptic, perfumed infusions, tinctures and herbal oils for toners and creams. The essential oil also comes from both leaves and flowers, and is used for sunburn antidotes and in relaxing baths.

non balm Use the leaves to make soothing, astringent infusions for cleansers.

ne Use the flowers and young leaves to make infusions for healing, moisturizing creams and lotions, and for hair-lightening rinses.

rigold Use the leaves and flowers to make healing infusions and decoctions for creams and lotions to treat oily skin, eczema and ageing skin. Also used for hair-lightening rinses.

rsh mallow Use the leaves and flowers to make softening, antiseptic infusions for creams and cleansers. Use the roots to make healing decoctions to treat problem skin.

nge blossom Use the essential oil in creams to soothe dry skin and skin with broken veins.

rsley Use crushed leaves or their extracted juice for healing poultices or lotions, or to make infusions for cleansers and creams to treat oily skins or skin with thread veins. Has anti-dandruff and deodorizing properties.

se Use the petals to make infusions, tinctures and oils for conditioning cleansers, toners, moisturizers and colognes. The essential oil also derives from the petals.

semary Use the leaves and flowers to make therapeutic infusions for all cosmetic preparations. Use the leaves to make herbal oils to massage into the hair and body. Has antiseptic, anti-dandruff properties.

ge Use the leaves and flowers to make healing, astringent infusions for cleansers and tonics to treat oily skin, and hair conditioners.

me Use the leaves to make astringent infusions and strongly perfumed herbal oils for soothing body rubs. Has deodorizing and anti-dandruff properties.

rrow Use the leaves or pounded flowers to make healing, astringent infusions for cleansers, face packs, steamers and creams to treat oily skin.

DRYING HERBS

When you are gathering herbs from your garden, try to avoid picking them when they are damp to minimize the risk of mould growing while they are tied together to dry. Hang separate bunches of the different herbs together upside down in a warm, dry place – away from direct sunlight and steam. They are ready for use when the leaves are easily crumbled.

A smaller quantity of herbs can be dried by placing the leaves in a round glass container and leaving it in a sunny spot. This method also works well with flower petals.

Strip the leaves from the stem of dried herbs and either store in closed jars or powder them by rubbing through your fingers. In the case of coarse herbs like rosemary, run them briefly through an electric blender.

THE BASIC ESSENTIALS

Most of the flower waters, infusions and oils mentioned in this book can be obtained from good herbalists. You will derive great satisfaction, however, from creating your own preparations, but it is essential that you are completely at home with the basic methods of preparation before you launch into production.

Ideally, you should aim to create a mini-workshop for the exclusive purpose of cosmetic manufacture, keeping your utensils and ingredients apart from your everyday kitchen equipment and supplies. If this is not possible, then ensure that all the utensils you need are scrupulously cleaned before use. Never use aluminium equipment because it will taint the preparations.

The essential herbal recipes

Herbal infusions, decoctions, vinegars, extracts, oils and essences and flower waters are used in cosmetic preparations to add fragrance or for their therapeutic properties. Whenever they are used, a preservative such as tincture of benzoin must be added to the recipe, because these natural compounds are perishable.

WHAT YOU WILL NEED

- ☐ Several heat-resistant glass or china bowls
- ☐ A *bain-marie* – a large saucepan or roasting pan containing water, in which the bowls can be placed to be heated to a regulated temperature.
- ☐ Scales
- ☐ A measuring jug
- ☐ A range of measuring spoons
- ☐ A wooden spoon and plastic spatula for mixing
- ☐ A pestle and mortar or stout china bowl and wooden "masher"

- ☐ A grater
- ☐ A fine nylon sieve
- ☐ A small electric whisk and liquidizer
- ☐ A small funnel
- ☐ An eyedropper or pipette
- ☐ Filter paper
- ☐ Kitchen paper
- ☐ Several suitable sterile dark glass jars and bottles with plastic-lined screw-top lids for storage – available from hardware stores.

**The ml and g conversions are given to the nearest 25.
The tablespoon and teaspoon measurements are 15ml and 5ml respectively.**

INFUSIONS

Basically, infusions are strong teas, using either herbs or flowers as a base. They are best made in china teapots – never use an aluminium pot as it will taint the infusion. Keep for no longer than three days in the refrigerator.

100g (4oz) of fresh or 50g (2oz) of dried herbs or flowers
575ml (1pt) purified water

Place the herbs in the teapot and pour in the freshly boiled water. Cover and leave to stand for three hours. Strain through filter paper before using.

Milk infusions can be added to basic milk cleansers or face masks to give them mild curative properties.

50g (2oz) fresh or 25g (1oz) of dried herbs or flowers
275ml (½pt) milk

Place the herbs in a large cup and cover with the cold milk. Place the saucer over the top and leave for 4 hours. Strain and use immediately.

FLOWER WATERS

You make flower waters using exactly the same method as that used for making infusions, though in this case the liquid should be left to stand overnight. Elderflower and rose make particularly good scented waters.

DECOCTIONS

The method used for extracting the maximum amount of goodness from the roots, bark and seeds of many herbs. Keep for no longer than three days in a refrigerator.

100g (4oz) fresh herbs
575ml (1pt) purified water

Gently boil the herbs and water together in a covered stainless steel or enamel pan. Simmer on a very gentle heat for at least one hour, but preferably for three, by which time the liquid should have reduced by one quarter. Strain through filter paper.

HERB EXTRACTS AND TINCTURES

These are invaluable in the making of concentrated herbal lotions and creams which last well. They are expensive to make, but well worth your initial outlay for the benefits they bring.

100g (4oz) of fresh herbs or flowers
575ml (1pt) pure alcohol
tincture of benzoin

Crush the herbs or flowers and place them in a jar. Cover with the alcohol, seal and leave in full sunlight, shaking daily for a week. Strain the mixture, pressing firmly, through filter paper and retain the liquid. Repeat the process with some fresh herbs or flowers, until the mixture has a good strong fragrance. Add a few drops of tincture of benzoin to ensure that it will last. Bottle and seal tightly. Store in a dark place.

HERB AND FLOWER ESSENCE

These essences are used to make herb and floral waters. Add 15ml (1 tablespoon) of the essence to 575ml (1 pint) of purified water.

15ml (1 tbsp) essential herb or flower oil
575ml (1pt) pure alcohol, wine or cider vinegar, or
* surgical spirit.*

Shake the ingredients together in a bottle and leave for several days before using.

HERB OR FLOWER OIL

The oils given here do not have the strength of essential oils, but they are both fragrant and therapeutic. They are cheap to make and can be used lavishly in massage and tanning oils and as a substitute for plain oils. A fine oil such as wheatgerm or almond may be substituted for the alcohol when making small quantities of a herbal oil for specific purposes.

50g (2oz) fresh or 25g (1oz) dried herbs or flower petals
575ml (1 pt) sunflower or olive oil
15ml (1 tbsp) pure alcohol or cider vinegar

Crush the herbs or petals with a little of the oil in a mortar with a pestle. Transfer to a large glass jar and add the remainder of the oil and the alcohol or vinegar. Seal tightly and shake well. Leave on a sunny windowsill and shake daily. If it is winter or there is no sunshine then stand the jar on an inverted saucer in a deep saucepan and submerge it to the level of the oil in warm water. Heat gently on a very low, regulated heat for an hour. Repeat daily.

After two weeks, strain the mixture, mashing it well through a nylon sieve. Repeat the process using the same quantity of fresh herbs or petals. Repeat the process until the oil has a good warm fragrance. You should not need to repeat it more than twice. Strain, bottle and seal.

HERB AND FLOWER VINEGARS

Herb and flower vinegars are very therapeutic – both rose and elderflower, for instance, relieve the tension of headaches. They are also used in astringents and hair rinses. The best vinegar to add to the bath is one made from a wide selection of herbs and flowers.

50g (2oz) of fresh or 25g (1oz) of dried herbs or flower
* petals*
575ml (1pt) cider or wine vinegar – never use malt
* vinegar*

If you are using dried herbs or petals, moisten them by pounding them in a little vinegar with a pestle and mortar. Warm a large plastic-lidded glass jar, then spoon in the herbs or petals. Heat the vinegar until just hot and pour it gradually into the jar. Seal tightly and shake well. Leave in a warm or sunny spot and shake daily for one month. Strain, re-bottle and seal.

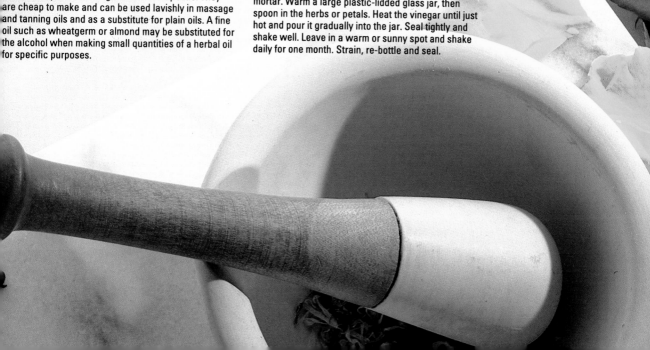

CHAPTER TWO

FACE FACTS

Caring for your skin properly depends on a thorough understanding of its structure and its tendencies regarding sensitivity, oiliness and fragility. When you feel sure that you are familiar with your skin's peculiarities, you can decide which natural beauty products to use and begin to establish a regular beauty routine, comprising thorough cleansing, toning, moisturizing, massage, exfoliation and steam cleansing.

Your eyes and your mouth deserve special attention because they are particularly sensitive and are your most important facial features. Your hair should be treated carefully using mild shampoos, conditioners, rinses and colorants to make it shine with natural health. It is as important to understand why your hair behaves as it does as it is to understand your skin's tendencies. To help you in both cases, this chapter includes charts of hair and skin types and problems which might affect those different types, together with the relevant recommended treatments.

Knowing your skin, how it functions and how to keep it looking at its best, no matter how old you are, is a matter of common sense. Understanding its construction will help to build confidence in coping with problem skins and improving upon and maintaining a well-balanced skin.

The skin is composed of three layers. The first layer, the *epidermis*, which is very thin and has no blood cells or nerves, is divided into an upper and basal layer. The upper layer is composed of skin cells formed by the protein *keratin*, the same hard substance of which your nails are made.

Skin problems usually arise in the upper layer of the epidermis because either the skin has not been cleansed sufficiently to remove make-up, thus causing the flakes of dead skin to matt together, or by using an over-harsh cleansing method, which has caused the skin to crack. In both cases, the skin is left open to infection.

Melanin cells, which cause freckles and deepen the skin's colour by responding to the ultraviolet rays in sunlight, are also found in the epidermis and act to protect the living tissue from sun damage.

The basal layer of the epidermis is where new skin cells are formed and nourished from the dermis beneath. If that nourishment is neglected, then healthy skin cells will not form and the skin will be dull and lifeless.

This cross section of a piece of skin tissue shows just how delicate its structure is. Skin is easily damaged – see how thin the **epidermis** is in relation to the two other major layers of tissue – so treating it with care is vitally important.

No two skins are ever the same. You will find that your own skin's requirements will change as you mature and in accordance with environmental conditions. Natural cosmetic therapy will help you cope with these variations.

Melanin cell

Sebaceous gland

Keratin

Hair shaft

Hair follicle

Freckle

Sweat gland

Epidermis

Dermis

Subcutaneous fat

Nerve endings

Blood capillaries

The *dermis* is the second skin layer. It is made up of fibrous tissue, sebaceous glands and hair follicles, blood vessels and nerve endings. The fibrous tissue is composed mainly of *collagen* and *elastin*. As the skin matures, these proteins harden and cause surface wrinkling. Sebaceous glands situated at the base of hair follicles, spread an even film of oil out across the skin through tiny invisible hairs. The oil is slightly acid and it is this "acid mantle" which protects the skin from bacteria. How abundantly and where the oil is secreted determines the skin type.

Blackheads, spots and acne often arise from overactive sebaceous glands producing too much oil and blocking the follicle exit, or pore. Minute blood vessels located in the dermis carry nourishment to the skin and remove waste matter. The purer their contents are, the healthier your skin will be.

Blood vessels are also reponsible for colour changes in the skin. Heat and emotion cause them to expand and turn the skin red; cold or shock causes them to contract and the skin turns white; nausea causes bile to travel to the skin's surface through the blood vessels, turning it 'green". When expanded blood vessels can no longer contract, small thread veins appear on the surface of the skin. Blemishes such as these, caused by damage to the dermis, can disappear, for providing the body is in good health the skin has remarkable recuperative powers. The nerve endings in the dermis are affected by temperature, touch and pain, so be aware of the skin's warning signals which will alert you to any potential problems.

Beneath the dermis is a layer of fat which immediately affects the quality of our skin's appearance. If there is too much fat or water retention in the skin's tissue, it will become uneven and lumpy causing the skin to stretch and dimple. However, a dramatic loss of weight can be just as unsightly as the stretched skin will sag, particularly if it has lost its elasticity, as it will in maturity.

This then is your skin. Your appearance and sense of well-being depend on how well you understand it, the thoroughness of your beauty routine and the quality of your cosmetics.

Bad reactions

A skin allergy is an adverse skin reaction to a foreign substance – dust, pollen, food and detergents are common examples of reactive allergens. People who suffer from food allergies, hay fever and asthma are the most prone to adverse reactions to cosmetic preparations. The allergy may

POSSIBLE TROUBLEMAKERS

There is no guarantee that any given ingredient will not cause an allergic reaction. What is important is being able to identify it – an impossible task if you use commercial cosmetic products containing synthetic substances.

Irritations will normally appear on your face, where the skin is far more sensitive than that on your hands or body. It could be a reaction to any one of these commonly used ingredients:

Almond oil
Avocado
Camphor
Cocoa butter
Glycerine
Lanolin
Oranges
Strawberries
Tinctures of benzoin and myrrh
Mineral powders or crystals, including sulphur and zinc
Essential oils

not manifest itself immediately on contact with a reactive substance and will show only after the skin has recognized a problem and produced the appropriate antibodies in order to combat it.

The first sign of your skin becoming sensitized is an unpleasant, red irritation which may become swollen, blistered or, in severe cases, develop into an open, flaking form of eczema. People who constantly suffer from allergies should test any new product before using it. No particular skin type suffers predominantly from allergic reactions, although fine and sensitive skins do react badly when harsh soaps and astringents are used on them, becoming tight, inflamed and irritated – conditions usually associated with allergy. As soon as your skin signals an allergy to a home-made preparation, investigate the cause immediately by patch testing *(see right)*, each ingredient used, so as to isolate the one causing the problem. Once you have found it, discard it straightaway.

Bear in mind that not all skin reactions relate directly to cosmetics. Animal hair, plastic or plants may all contain allergens which have been unwittingly transferred to your skin, so if you cannot identify the cause immediately cast your net wider. If it appears an insoluble or painfully persistent problem seek professional medical advice.

Recognition and treatment

Not all adverse skin reactions are the direct result of contact with an allergenic substance. Your skin can develop the blotchiness usually associated with an allergic reaction as a result of increased stress, tension, heat, or haste, so never use a new preparation before a special occasion. The product may not be allergenic, but your skin could react as if it were.

The moment unwanted symptoms appear, cleanse the affected area thoroughly with plenty of clean cool water to lower the temperature of the skin and remove the potentially reactive substance. If the condition persists and the skin is uncomfortably taut, itching or inflamed then it must be eased quickly to avoid increased distress which will only exacerbate the problem.

A sterile gauze pad soaked in an infusion of comfrey and camomile, squeezed out and applied to the affected area should bring relief. Witch hazel can also be used, but is not always as effective. Try not to wear any make-up for a while and spray your skin with water to cool and moisturize it. It is most important that you do not scratch the rash and risk infecting it.

To make a patch test:
Take a small strip of sticking plaster. Place a little of the substance you are testing on the gauze padding and tape it firmly to either the soft skin on your inner arm beneath the elbow joint, or behind your ear. Providing the different tests are easily distinguishable, you can make several tests at once. Leave the plaster on your skin for 24 hours by which time it will have reacted.

SKIN DEEP

A sympathetic understanding of your skin and its needs is essential to good skin care and ultimately a beautiful complexion. There are several different skin types, each of which requires specific preparations and routines to keep it healthy, radiant and problem-free. The following simple test provides an instant indication of your skin type – a more detailed analysis is given in the chart *(see right)*.

When you first get up in the morning, stand in good light and press one sheet of a double tissue against your face. (It is important that you have cleaned your face thoroughly the night before.) Examine the tissue in the light. Any transparent marks on the tissue are evidence of oil – this indicates an oily skin. If there are traces of oil only in the central section of your face, this means you have a combination skin, that is, oily in the centre and dry on the cheeks. If there are no traces of oil at all, you have dry skin. Problem skin is prone to blemishes, spots, blackheads and open pores. Its texture is sometimes rough.

Every type of skin – even apparently perfect skin – needs careful cleansing and nourishing, not only for the short-term benefits of clear skin, but also to make sure that it does not age prematurely. Inadequate skin care can do irreparable damage, even though it may not be apparent when you are young. The effects of age usually begin to show after you reach 30 and after this age, even more meticulous skin care is needed.

Age is not the skin's only enemy. Pollution, central heating, air-conditioning, sun, wind and rain also have a very detrimental effect on your skin, drying it and ageing it more quickly than would happen otherwise. For this reason, it is important that you protect your skin as much as possible against these harmful factors when necessary, and give it extra nourishment to restore the natural oils it has lost.

You should remember that the condition of your skin is also governed from within, and it is therefore vital that you eat a balanced, healthy diet (avoid sugars and fats in particular), drink plenty of water, and have enough sleep. The improvement in your skin condition will enhance your natural beauty, whether you wear make-up or go bare-faced.

RECOGNIZING SKIN TYPES

DRY SKIN

Dry skin feels rough and papery to the touch; it also wrinkles easily. This type of skin is usually very thin and may age prematurely unless carefully looked after. It reacts badly to harsh winds or changes in temperature. Make-up tends to stand out and face powder looks floury.

OILY SKIN

Oily skin is characteristically shiny and coarse in texture; the pores are usually enlarged, while blackheads and the occasional spot are common. Make-up does not last well, and your foundation tends to become yellow.

COMBINATION SKIN

Combination skin means exactly that – your cheeks will be dry, while the centre panel of your face is shiny and open-pored. Quite often your skin feels rough. The dry areas are sensitive to sun, wind and harsh soaps, while your make-up disappears quickly in the oily patches.

PROBLEM SKIN

Your skin produces too much oil, making it shiny and prone to acne. This is usually caused by hormonal problems. If the acne is acute you should consult a doctor or a dermatologist for treatment.

AGEING SKIN

The condition of every skin type deteriorates with age. Dry skin becomes prone to wrinkles, particularly around the eyes, and broken veins appear. Oily skin becomes coarser and dull in appearance.

CLEANSING	TONING	NOURISHING
Always use creamy cleansers or mild skin milks, as they have a thicker consistency than those made for oily skins. Avoid washing with soap and water as these aggravate the dryness. Apply the cleanser smoothly over your face and neck and remove with tissues or cotton wool.	Use a mild skin tonic on a pad of cotton wool moistened with cold water. This tightens and tones your skin and will also stimulate the circulation. Use a cream face mask once a week.	You must use a nourishing cream after cleansing your face at night to replace the moisture that you have just removed. Massage in the cream and remove any surplus after 15 minutes, by which time your skin will have absorbed all the moisture it needs.
Oily skin demands thorough regular cleansing. You should always cleanse your skin twice to make sure that you have removed all surface grime. Use an astringent cleansing milk and plenty of cotton wool, or wash your face using a cream that contains pore-refining grains.	Your skin needs stimulation to help it slough off dead cells. Use an exfoliating cream or a complexion sponge twice a week if you suffer from open pores and blackheads. Apply an astringent face mask once a week. Before you you apply any make-up, prepare your skin with a gentle astringent.	Use grease-free creams and lotions to discourage bacteria and promote healing. Do not neglect delicate areas, such as the skin around the eyes. Use a light moisturizing cream at night after cleansing thoroughly and toning.
Use a creamy cleanser every morning, or wash your face with herbal soap and softened water. If washing aggravates your dry cheeks, cleanse them separately and wash only the oily panels with the herbal soap and water. Use a cream cleanser every evening.	Tone your cheeks with a mild skin tonic on a pad of damp cotton wool. Use an exfoliating cream twice a week to refine the skin in the centre panel. Once a week, apply a mild face pack to your cheeks, with a more astringent mask down the centre panel of your face.	Every evening after cleansing pat a night cream, formulated for dry skin, on your cheeks. Use an oil-free moisturizer on these areas every morning before applying your make-up. Smooth a corrective lotion or anti-blackhead cream on the centre panel.
It is vital that you keep your skin, hair, brushes, combs, towels and pillowcases scrupulously clean. Otherwise you will only aggravate the problem. To cleanse your face, wash it with a pure soap.	Draw out the impurities in your skin instead of just drying its surface – tone with a herbal extractive cream. In extreme cases, when the acne is very bad, it is worth asking your doctor if it can be treated with an infrared lamp.	You must ensure that every product you use matches your cleanser – it is pointless to use an extractive toner and a drying astringent, since one will cancel out the effect of the other. Apply moisturizer as for an oily skin.
For dry skin, use a rich cleansing milk; for oily skin, use a mild soap. For combination skin, use a gentle cleansing milk daily and a mild soap twice a week.	Tone dry skin with mineral water or gentle toner. For oily skin, use an astringent, washing grains, and a clay mask once a week. For combination skin, use a gentle toner and a mild exfoliant once a week.	For dry skin, use a rich, nourishing night cream and an oil-based moisturizer during the day. Use an oil-free moisturizer on oily skin. For dual skin, you must use an oil-based moisturizer on the dry areas, and an oil-free moisturizer on the oily areas.

Skin care/1

No matter what skin type you have, it must be thoroughly cleansed at the beginning and end of each day. The professional method of cleansing the skin employs movements which work against the grain of lines and wrinkles, thereby improving the elasticity of the skin. Use a cotton wool pad for milk, lotion or oil cleansers and your fingertips for cream cleansers.

Use firm upward strokes to clean your throat and cheeks, small circling movements to clean from your chin up to your temples, up and down strokes on your forehead, lateral strokes across the lip and chin area and around the eyes, swirling strokes moving from the outer cheek in across the bone beneath the eyes, in towards the nose and up across the brow. Allow half a minute for the cleanser to penetrate and remove with tissues using the same movements.

1 Apply cleanser to the back of your hands and work them up from the base of your throat to your chin with long firm strokes.

2 With your second and third fingers, move over your chin to work along your jawbone using small circling movements. Continue ▷ up over your cheeks towards your temples.

3 Move across your forehead working your second and third fingers gently up and down.

◁

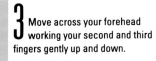

30

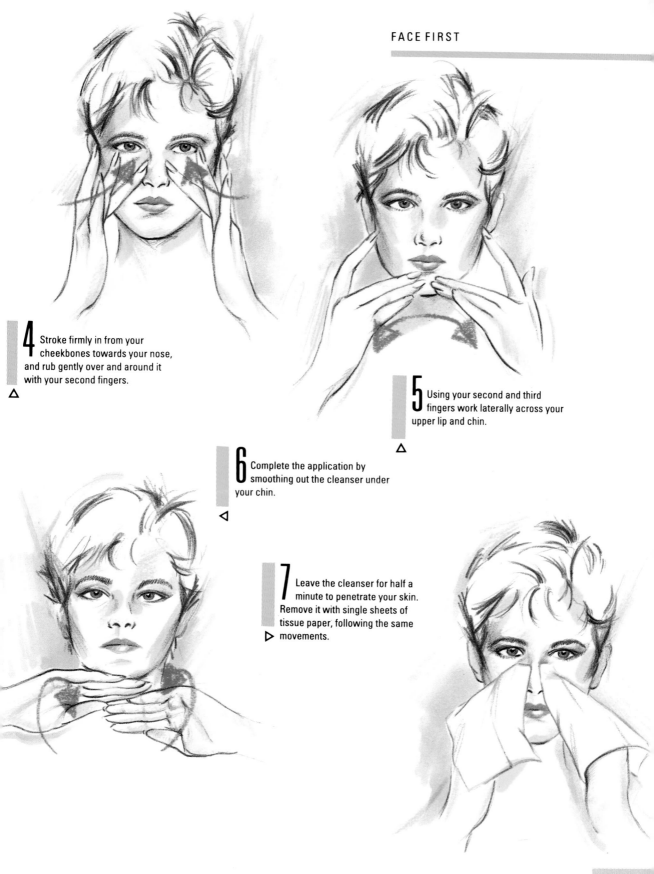

4 Stroke firmly in from your cheekbones towards your nose, and rub gently over and around it with your second fingers.

5 Using your second and third fingers work laterally across your upper lip and chin.

6 Complete the application by smoothing out the cleanser under your chin.

7 Leave the cleanser for half a minute to penetrate your skin. Remove it with single sheets of tissue paper, following the same movements.

SKIN CARE/2

CLEANSERS

Really thorough cleansing is a must if you wear make-up during the day, or if you have made your face up specially for a party. The pores of your skin can become clogged and infected if every trace of make-up is not removed, resulting in spots or inflammation. A soothing cleanse is a very relaxing way to end the day, and acts as an instant freshener first thing in the morning.

SIMPLE SECRETS

Dry and normal skins:
Almond, avocado, sunflower or olive oil, milk and buttermilk.

Oily skins:
Yoghurt, a paste of skimmed dried milk or ground unprocessed oatmeal mixed with cream or milk. Extracted fruit and vegetable juice — strawberry, cucumber, lemon.

Problem skins:
Herbal infusions made with milk or water.

Tired skins:
Vegetable waters — spinach, cabbage, potato, carrot.

BASIC CLEANSING CREAM

This basic recipe is for a simple, light cleansing cream, suitable for all skin types.

13ml (½oz) white wax
90ml (6 tbsps) almond oil
75ml (5 tbsps) purified water
1.25ml (¼ tsp) borax
4 drops essential oil or perfumed water
2 drops tincture of benzoin

Mix the melted wax and oil together and warm them in a bowl at an even, low heat in a *bain-marie* until they have combined. Heat the purified water to the same temperature in a separate bowl, also in the *bain-marie*. Using a wooden spoon, beat the water into the wax mixture, with the borax to prevent separation. Essential oils or perfumed water could be substituted for the purified water to provide fragrance, if desired. Add a few drops of tincture of benzoin to act as a preservative – a particularly necessary step if you have chosen to substitute home-made herbal infusions or decoctions for the purified water (see pp20-1).

When the ingredients are all mixed, beat the mixture continuously until it is thick, cool and in no danger of separating. Spoon it into 150ml (¼pt) container and seal.

COCOA BUTTER AND LANOLIN CLEANSER

A rich, oily and gentle cleansing cream, suitable for sun or wind dried and ageing skins.

60ml (4 tbsps) almond oil
2.5ml (½ tbsp) anhydrous lanolin
2.5ml (½ tbsp) cocoa butter
1.25ml (¼ tsp) borax
30ml (2 tbsps) rosewater

Melt the oil, lanolin and cocoa butter together in a bowl in a *bain-marie*. Dissolve the borax in a bowl with the gently heating rosewater. Remove both bowls from the heat and beat the rosewater mixture into the oils. Continue beating until the mixture cools and thickens. Spoon into a 150ml (¼pt) pot, seal and label.

COMFREY CLEANSING CREAM

A gentle, healing and soothing cleansing cream, suitable for dry and sensitive skins.

150ml (¼ pt) almond, sunflower or olive oil
13g (½ oz) beeswax
30ml (2 tbsps) cocoa butter
150ml (¼ pt) strong comfrey infusion (see p20)
5ml (1 tsp) borax
10ml (2 tsps) clear honey
2 drops tincture of benzoin

Melt the oil, beeswax and cocoa butter together in a bowl in a *bain-marie*. Heat the infusion in a second bowl to the same temperature and add the borax and honey, stirring well until they dissolve. Remove both bowls from the heat and beat the comfrey mixture with the benzoin into the oils. Continue beating until the mixture cools and thickens. Spoon into a 425ml (¾pt) pot, seal and label. Keep refrigerated.

APPLE CLEANSING LOTION

A soothing and deep cleansing lotion, suitable for all skin types.

1 apple
15ml (1 tbsp) milk
15ml (1 tbsp) fuller's earth

Extract the juice from the apple with a juice extractor, or by mashing and sieving, and combine it with the other ingredients. Use for one application only.

ELDERFLOWER AND BUTTERMILK CLEANSER

A mildly bleaching, cooling and softening cleansing lotion, suitable for dry skins.

300ml (½ pt) buttermilk
50g (2oz) fresh or 25g (1oz) dried elderflowers

Simmer the milk and elderflowers together for 30 minutes. Remove from the heat, cover and infuse for two hours. Strain, bottle and keep refrigerated.
Note: For an almond milk cleanser, also suitable for dry skins, substitute 60ml (4 tbsps) of ground almonds for the elderflowers.

YOGHURT AND LEMON CLEANSING MILK

A cleansing, antiseptic and bleaching cleansing lotion, suitable for oily skins.

15ml (1 tbsp) natural yoghurt
5ml (1 tsp) pure lemon juice

Mix the two ingredients together and use for one application only.

SKIN CARE/3

TONERS AND REFRESHERS

You need toners, fresheners and astringents to remove all traces of your cleanser, to tighten pores, brighten the skin and to restore its acidity level, which is inevitably altered by cleansing and washing.

Toners are designed to be gentle and this is reflected in the ingredients used to make them. They contain rosewater or soothing herbal infusions, natural astringents and glycerine, and are ideal for dry and sensitive skins.

Fresheners are also mild, but they contain slightly more stimulating ingredients. The skin-tingling herbs, lemon juice and cider or herb vinegars which they contain will refresh a well-balanced skin.

Astringents, as their name suggests, are far stronger. They are largely made up of natural astringents or alcohol, which dissolve natural oil and reduce enlarged pores. They are therefore only suitable for oily skins.

These lotions may be applied in two ways — on well-saturated cotton wool pads, or poured into atomizers and sprayed in a fine dew onto the skin.

SIMPLE SECRETS

The simplest fresheners are those based on infusions of herbs and flowers *(see p20)*, but there are other very straightforward basic recipes.

Oily skins:
Elderflower or parsley infusion.
Two drops of camphor added to rinsing water.

Normal and oily skins:
Half a cucumber, liquidized and strained.

Problem skins:
Marigold infusion.

Dry and ageing skins:
Mineral water.

Tired skins:
Cornflower infusion.

Windburnt or sunburnt skins:
Camomile infusion.

All skin types:
15ml (1 tablespoon) of vinegar added to rinsing water.

ROSEWATER AND WITCH HAZEL TONER

A cooling and soothing tonic lotion, suitable for dry and sensitive skins.

425ml (¾ pt) rosewater
150ml (¼ pt) witch hazel
2.5ml (½ tsp) glycerine

Combine all the ingredients in a bottle and shake well.

CUCUMBER AND MINT FRESHENER

A cooling, refreshing and stimulating refresher, suitable for balanced skins.

½ large cucumber
60ml (4 tbsps) chopped fresh mint
15ml (1 tbsp) witch hazel

Liquidize the cucumber and mint together. Strain and add the witch hazel to the resulting juice. Pour into a 150ml (¼pt) bottle, seal and keep refrigerated.

ELDERFLOWER FACE FRESHENER

A gentle, softening and antiseptic refresher, suitable for balanced or slightly sunburnt skins.

60ml (4 tbsps) elderflower infusion (see p20)
60ml (4 tbsps) glycerine
15ml (1 tbsp) orange flower water
7.5ml (½ tbsp) pure lemon juice

Combine all the ingredients together in a 150ml (¼pt) bottle and shake well. Keep refrigerated.

HERB VINEGAR RINSE

A rinse which restores the acid mantle, suitable for all skin types.

275ml (½ pt) herb vinegar (see p21)
275ml (½ pt) purified elderflower, orange flower or rosewater (see p20).

Mix the two liquids together. Bottle and add two tablespoons to a washbasin of cold water for rinsing the face.

LEMON AND PEPPERMINT ASTRINGENT

A stimulating and antiseptic astringent tonic, suitable for oily problem skins.

60ml (4 tbsps) fresh lemon juice
2.5ml (½ tsp) peppermint extract
150ml (¼ pt) witch hazel
30ml (2 tbsps) alcohol

Combine all the ingredients and leave to stand for 24 hours. Strain and pour into a 275ml (½pt) bottle.

LEMON BLEACHING TONIC

An astringent and bleaching lotion, suitable for fading tans and sallow skins.

½ lemon
150ml (¼ pt) white wine
5ml (1 tsp) white sugar

Slice the lemon and boil it in the wine for one minute. Stir in the sugar until it is dissolved. Leave to cool. Strain into a 150ml (¼pt) bottle and keep refrigerated.

MARIGOLD ASTRINGENT

A gently healing astringent tonic, suitable for problem skins.

150ml (¼ pt) marigold infusion (see p20)
15ml (1 tbsp) witch hazel

Combine the two liquids in a bottle, shake well and keep refrigerated.

SKIN CARE/4

MOISTURIZERS AND CONDITIONING CREAMS

You should moisturize your skin religiously if it is to maintain its elasticity and bloom. Moisturizers provide a thin protective film of oil and water over the skin's surface, which prevents the evaporation of the skin's natural moisture and replaces your skin's natural oils when these are depleted by climatic and living conditions, over-zealous cleansing or age.

Nourishing night creams reinforce the protective, conditioning action of a regularly applied moisturizer. Both sorts of cream should be applied after cleansing and toning, following the Facial Massage movements *(see pp38-9)*.

SIMPLE SECRETS
A very simple moisturizer is a thin film of fine vegetable oil spread over the skin, splashed with water and blotted dry.

BASIC MOISTURIZING CREAM

A light smooth cream, suitable for all skin types.

20ml (4 tsps) emulsifying wax
20ml (4 tsps) coconut oil
40ml (8 tsps) almond oil
90ml (6 tbsps) purified water

Melt the wax in a bowl in a *bain-marie* and beat in the oils. Bring the water to the same temperature in a separate bowl. Remove both bowls from the heat and beat the water into the oil and wax mixture. Continue beating until the mixture is cool. Add a few drops of your favourite perfume for fragrance. Use lavishly and keep refrigerated in a 150ml (¼pt) bottle.

This cream is designed to be adapted according to your tastes and requirements. The purified water and perfume can be substituted with various additives, but you must add two drops of tincture of benzoin to preserve the cream.

For an orange blossom moisturizer, add 90ml (6 tbsps) of orange flower water and perfume with oil of neroli or bergamot. This is a most effective rich cream, especially suitable for older skins or those exposed to sun and wind. It smoothes out dry skin and wrinkles.

For a strawberry moisturizer, add 90ml (6 tbsps) of strawberry juice and perfume with strawberry essence or rose geranium oil. This is suitable as a healing cream for oily skins, and for sunburnt or windburnt faces, throats and shoulders.

For a rich rose moisturizer add 90ml (6 tbsps) of rosewater and perfume with oil of roses. This is an exquisite soothing cream which is ideal for dry skins.

Herbal infusions may also be substituted for the purified water. Use lavender flower water, which is healing and antiseptic, and lavender oil for a fragrant moisturizer suitable for all skins. Elderflower, marigold and lime flowers are healing and make good moisturizers. Add a few drops of light floral perfume if you wish. Marsh mallow, comfrey and camomile infusions make gentle healing moisturizers perfumed with a few drops of camomile oil.

LIGHT NON-GREASY MOISTURIZER

A light and quickly absorbed lotion, suitable for normal and greasy skins.

30ml (2 tbsps) emulsifying wax
5ml (1 tsp) anhydrous lanolin
30ml (2 tbsps) sunflower, safflower or almond oil
120ml (8 tbsps) purified water
2.5ml (½ tsp) borax
7.5ml (1½ tsps) glycerine
5ml (1 tsp) witch hazel
perfumed oil – optional

Melt the wax and lanolin together in a bowl in a *bain-marie* and add the oil. Heat the water to the same temperature in a separate bowl and dissolve the borax in it. Add the glycerine and the witch hazel once the borax has dissolved. Remove both bowls from the heat and, beating constantly, slowly add the water to the wax mixture. Continue beating until the mixture is cool, adding a few drops of perfumed oil if desired. Spoon into a 250ml (9fl oz) pot.

ALMOND AND AVOCADO CREAM

A light and easily absorbed lotion, suitable for all skin types, even the most fragile.

5ml (1 tsp) beeswax
10ml (2 tsps) emulsifying wax
40ml (8 tsps) almond oil
20ml (4 tsps) avocado oil
30ml (2 tbsps) purified water
a pinch of borax
a few drops of perfumed oil

Melt the waxes together in a bowl in a *bain-marie* and add the oils. Heat the water at the same time and dissolve the borax in it. Remove both bowls from the heat and beat the water into the oils a little at a time. Continue beating until cool, then add a few drops of perfumed oil to the mixture if desired. Spoon into a 100ml (4fl oz) pot, seal and label.

BASIC COLD CREAM

Use the recipe given for the basic cleansing cream *(see p32)*, substituting either rose or rose petal water, elderflower or rosemary water for the purified water. All these have highly beneficial effects on the skin.

SUPERB ALL-PURPOSE CONDITIONING CREAM

A smooth and nourishing night cream, suitable for dry or normal skins.

60ml (4 tbsps) emulsifying wax
30ml (2 tbsps) beeswax
45ml (3 tbsps) anhydrous lanolin
60ml (4 tbsps) almond oil
60ml (4 tbsps) sesame oil
30ml (2 tbsps) avocado oil
60ml (4 tbsps) sunflower oil
75ml (5 tbsps) purified water
2.5ml (½ tsp) borax

Melt the waxes together in a bowl in a *bain-marie* and add the lanolin and oils. Heat the water to the same temperature in a separate bowl and stir the borax in until it dissolves. Remove both the bowls from the heat and slowly add the water to the oils, beating constantly. Beat gently until the mixture thickens and cools. Spoon into a 500ml (18fl oz)) pot and seal.

MARIGOLD AND WHEATGERM CREAM

A light, healing and nourishing night cream, particularly suitable for mature, blemished or climatically damaged skins.

30ml (2 tbsps) beeswax
30ml (2 tbsps) anhydrous lanolin
90ml (6 tbsps) almond oil
5ml (1 tsp) wheatgerm oil
90ml (6 tbsps) marigold infusion (see p20)
2.5ml (½ tsp) borax
2 drops tincture of benzoin

Melt the lanolin and wax together in a bowl in a *bain-marie* and add the oils. In a separate bowl, heat the marigold infusion to the same temperature and stir in the borax until it dissolves. Remove both the bowls from the heat and beat the marigold mixture with the benzoin slowly into the oils. Continue beating until thick and cool. Spoon into a 275ml (½pt) pot, seal and keep refrigerated.

HONEY AND LECITHIN CREAM

A nourishing and rejuvenating night cream, suitable for all skin types especially those which tend to look sallow.

10ml (2 tsps) anhydrous lanolin
30ml (2 tbsps) almond oil
7.5ml (½ tbsp) clear honey
30ml (2 tbsps) purified water
5ml (1 tsp) lecithin powder

Melt the lanolin in a bowl in a *bain-marie* and stir in the oil and honey. Warm the water in a second bowl to the same temperature. Remove both bowls from the heat and add the water to the lanolin mixture, beating well. Continue beating until cool and then add the lecithin, stirring well. Spoon into a 100ml (4fl oz) pot, seal and keep refrigerated.

RICH VITAMIN CREAM

A very nourishing and healing night cream which restores elasticity and improves the condition of all skin types.

15ml (1 tbsp) beeswax
15ml (1 tbsp) emulsifying wax
15ml (1 tbsp) anhydrous lanolin
30ml (2 tbsps) almond or sesame oil
45ml (3 tbsps) wheatgerm oil
90ml (6 tbsps) purified water
2.5ml (½ tsp) borax
4 capsules Vitamin A oil
2 drops tincture of benzoin

Melt the waxes and lanolin together in a bowl in a *bain-marie* and add the oils. Heat the water to the same temperature in a separate bowl and stir in the borax until it dissolves. Remove both bowls from the heat and add the water to the waxes and oils, beating constantly until the mixture begins to cool. Prick the Vitamin A capsules open and add to the mixture with the benzoin. Continue beating until thick and set. Spoon into a 425ml (¾pt) pot and seal.

SIMPLE STRAWBERRY CREAM

Strawberry juice reduces oiliness and improves skin colour. Other soft fruits, such as raspberries and blackberries, can be substituted for the strawberries to make night creams equally valuable in the treatment of oily skins. Raspberry cream, which contains healing Vitamin C, is especially useful for problem skins.

juice from 6 good-sized strawberries
30ml (2 tbsps) anhydrous lanolin
30ml (2 tbsps) sunflower oil

Obtain your juice by mashing fresh or frozen strawberries through a nylon sieve. Melt the lanolin and oil in a *bain-marie* and add the warmed juice, stirring well. Beat continuously until the mixture cools. Make a small amount of cream at a time and keep refrigerated.

MASSAGE MATTERS/1

When applying moisturizer in the morning or conditioner at night, take a little extra time to turn your beauty routine into a therapeutic massage treatment which will make you feel good both mentally and physically. Throughout history, beautiful women have recognized the beneficial effects of a regular facial massage. The whole routine described below takes no longer than 15 minutes and can be adapted to stimulate or relax you as you choose. If you cannot fit it in every day, then make sure you incorporate it into your weekly facial treatment *(see p45)*.

Regular facial massage stimulates your facial muscles and your circulation and therefore the flow of nutrients to the skin's cells, which in turn results in an improved skin elasticity and colour. The ageing process is delayed by this stimulating exercise.

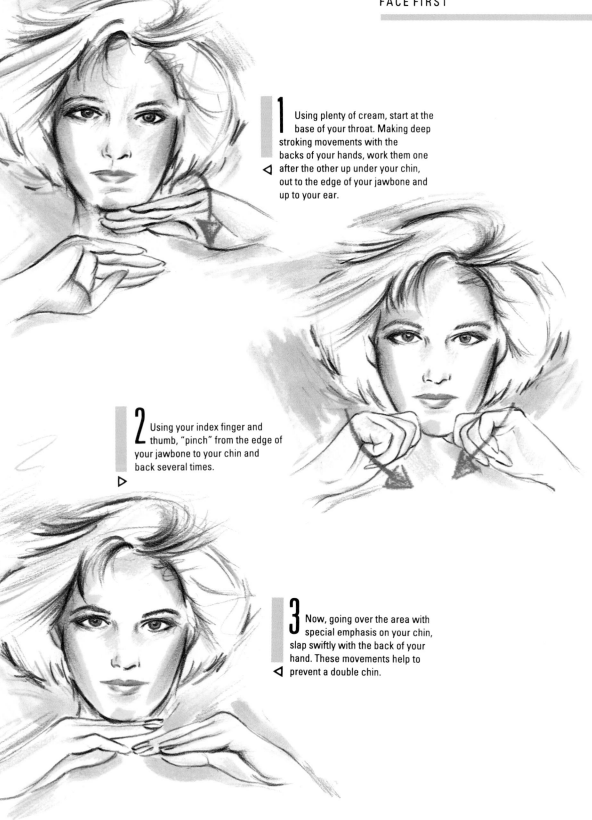

1 Using plenty of cream, start at the base of your throat. Making deep stroking movements with the backs of your hands, work them one after the other up under your chin, out to the edge of your jawbone and up to your ear.

2 Using your index finger and thumb, "pinch" from the edge of your jawbone to your chin and back several times.

3 Now, going over the area with special emphasis on your chin, slap swiftly with the back of your hand. These movements help to prevent a double chin.

MASSAGE MATTERS/2

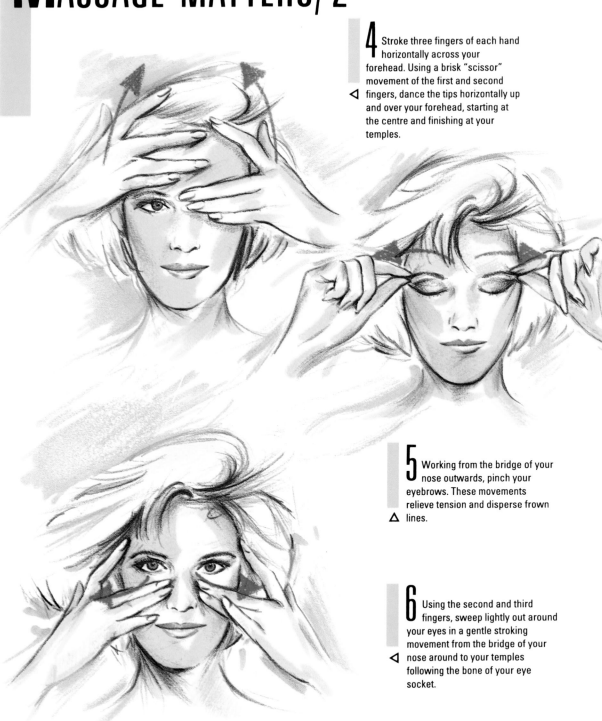

4 Stroke three fingers of each hand horizontally across your forehead. Using a brisk "scissor" movement of the first and second ◁ fingers, dance the tips horizontally up and over your forehead, starting at the centre and finishing at your temples.

5 Working from the bridge of your nose outwards, pinch your eyebrows. These movements relieve tension and disperse frown △ lines.

6 Using the second and third fingers, sweep lightly out around your eyes in a gentle stroking movement from the bridge of your ◁ nose around to your temples following the bone of your eye socket.

7 There are two pressure points, one at the bridge of your nose where it meets your eye socket and the other at your temple just level with the end of your eyebrow. Gentle pressure applied at these points with your fingertips and maintained for five seconds, will dispel a considerable amount of tension.

8 Move on to treat your cheek muscles by working from your chin up across your cheeks to your temples with an upwards circling movement of your fingertips. Work down your face to finish at your chin.

9 Finally, stroke your neck gently from your jaw down to your shoulder several times to relieve any tension.

NOTE:
Pinching, slapping, scissoring movements and relieving tension at given pressure points can be done in private at any time of the day to stimulate the circulation and relax you.

CLEANER THAN CLEAN

SKIN POLISHERS

Dead skin cells which remain on the skin's surface for too long give the skin a dull appearance and can, in some cases, be a cause of infection. They should be regularly removed with facial scrubs or exfoliators. The small circular movements of your fingertips or a complexion brush, used to apply these gently abrasive scrubs, stimulate the skin, improving the circulation and toning slack muscles as they clean. Polishing your skin in this way will promote a smooth, glowing complexion.

Dry, sensitive skins benefit from a mild facial scrub once a week, while oily skins will improve with more regular treatments. All facial scrubs should be left on the skin for a few minutes after application. Once you feel you have massaged the scrub well over your skin, rinse it off with tepid water and smooth on some moisturizer.

SIMPLE SECRETS

Dry skins:
15ml (1 tablespoon) of ground almonds mixed to a paste with clear honey.

Dry and sensitive skins:
15ml (1 tablespoon) of wheatgerm mixed to a paste with cream.

Oily skins:
15ml (1 tablespoon) of sugar mixed with soap lather.
Salt gently applied on a face cloth.

Oily and problem skins:
Mashed strawberries.

WHEATGERM AND HONEY SCRUB

A soothing and smoothing scrub, suitable for dry and patchy skins.

15ml (1 tbsp) wheatgerm
10ml (2 tsps) clear honey
5ml (1 tsp) almond oil
5ml (1 tsp) fresh lemon juice.

Mix all the ingredients together to form a stiff paste.

MARIGOLD AND YOGHURT PASTE

A healing and cleansing scrub, suitable for blemished and ageing skins and those exposed to sun and wind.

15ml (1 tbsp) fresh or 7.5ml (½ tbsp) dried marigold petals
5ml (1 tsp) wheatgerm oil
5ml (1 tsp) clear honey
15ml (1 tbsp) plain yoghurt
5ml (1 tsp) fresh lemon juice

Pound the marigold petals with the oil and honey in a pestle and mortar. Add the yoghurt and lemon juice and leave to stand for a few minutes before using.

BRAN AND YOGHURT SCRUB

An abrasive and healing scrub, suitable for blemished skins.

30ml (2 tbsps) bran
5ml (1 tsp) fine sea salt
plain yoghurt

Mix the bran and salt with enough yoghurt to make a thick paste.

ORANGE AND ALMOND SCRUB

A mildly abrasive scrub, suitable for normal skins.

15ml (1 tbsp) finely chopped dried orange peel
15ml (1 tbsp) ground almonds
15ml (1 tbsp) finely ground oatmeal

Mix all the ingredients with enough milk or water to make a paste.

STEAM CLEAN

The use of a steam facial is undoubtedly the most effective way to deep-cleanse your skin. Ideally, you should treat yourself to one every week in conjunction with a face mask. Steaming relaxes your skin, encouraging it to release impurities and, at the same time, stimulating the release of nutrients to the skin cells and the removal of toxins.

The addition of herbs to the moist atmosphere of a steam facial has a variety of therapeutic as well as cosmetic effects. Herbs heal, soothe, cleanse, stimulate, dry and tighten the skin. Some are effective in drawing spots to a head, others for loosening blackheads, but at all times they are calmative and relaxing. Use herbs either individually or in mixed bunches to suit your own skin type *(see pp18-19)*.

Although a steam facial is considered beneficial for all skin types, I would advise against using one if your skin is very dry or sensitive, or has visible thread veins. Steam treatments can also exacerbate skins suffering from pustular acne, and should *never* be used by asthmatics or people suffering from other breathing difficulties.

For a herbal steamer

Cover your hair and thoroughly cleanse your face *(see pp30-1)*. Place two handfuls of the appropriate herb or herbs in a large bowl and cover them with a litre (2 pints) of boiling water. Hold your face at least 30cm (12 ins) above the water and cover your head and the bowl with a thick towel to prevent the steam escaping. Stay under the towel for 10 minutes. Continue your facial by applying a face mask, or simply blot your face dry and refresh it with tepid water or a toner, followed by a moisturizer.

Do not subject your face to a cold atmosphere until your skin has cooled down.

Facial facts/1

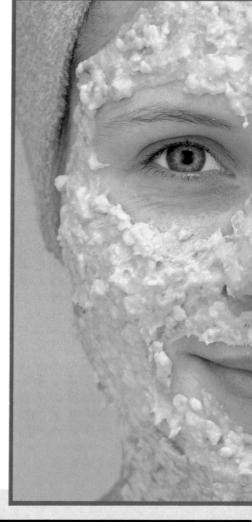

All skin benefits from the regular application of a face mask, which cleanses and stimulates. They improve the circulation, which in turn encourages a healthy flow of nutrients to the skin, thereby enhancing its tone, texture and colour. However, face masks can benefit the skin in other ways too. Some are healing, with a deep drawing action to remove impurities from problem skins, while others rejuvenate tired or mature skins. There are masks you can make to moisturize, bleach and tone your skin as and when it seems to need them.

The finest masks are made from fruit, vegetables and herbs which contain a relatively high proportion of natural vitamins, minerals, acids, antiseptics and oils. The most commonly used fruits are those that can be applied directly to the face — apples, peaches, apricots, plums, strawberries, grapes, bananas, pineapple, avocado, tomato, even paw-paw and mango, and of course the invaluable juices of oranges and lemons. Raw grated vegetables such as carrots or cucumber and cooked root vegetables are often used for beauty treatments, but it is more often the extracted or infused vegetable juices that are used.

Warm mashed poultices of herbs combined with a thickening agent, or herbal infusions added to basic dry ingredients make remedial and soothing masks.

The thickening agents used to bind masks vary from cooked rice and chickpeas, to oatmeal, fuller's earth and

Natural yoghurt mixed with fresh cucumber *(right)*, and ripe avocado flesh mashed to a paste with home-made mayonnaise *(above right)*, make tonic, moisturizing masks.

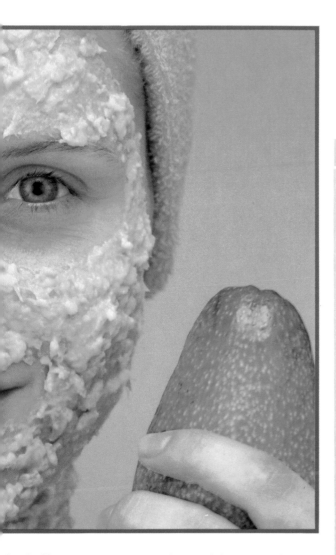

kaolin. Honey, cream, eggs, yoghurt and vinegar are also used to nourish, tighten or bleach your skin.

Follow your instincts

Experiment with the various ingredients to find the perfect face mask. On a day when your skin looks grey and greasy, a mask of strawberries and cream will improve it no end; when your skin looks as dull and tired as you feel, a warm and soothing mask of camomile will gently revive it, as will a saturated gauze compress of mint tea or pineapple juice on a hot, sticky summer's day.

When inventing your own recipes, remember that a mask should be just thin enough to smooth on the face without dragging the skin, yet thick enough to stay in place. Very liquid masks can be applied with a soft 12mm (½in) paintbrush. Most masks require 15-20 minutes' drying time, unless otherwise stated in the recipe, and should be rinsed off with tepid water.

THE PERFECT FACIAL

A facial once a week, incorporating the use of a face mask, is the most effective way of ensuring a thoroughly cleansed and healthy skin. Using natural ingredients in the mask enables you to make the right choice for the condition of your skin at any particular time, depending on whether it needs to be nourished, deeply cleansed, moisturized or revitalized.

Tie your hair back from your face.

Thoroughly remove make-up with a cleanser *(see pp30-31)*.

Prepare a herbal steam bath *(see p43)*. This is an optional step, but is particularly beneficial when a really deep cleansing is required. Blot the skin dry after steaming.

Apply the face mask. This must be done gently using the fingertips and taking great care not to drag the skin. Avoid the sensitive areas around the eyes and mouth.

Cover the eyes with gauze pads soaked in a mild skin tonic *(see p34)*, or suitable herbal infusion *(see p20)*, to soothe and cool.

Lie down for the prescribed time according to which mask you have used, relax and refuse to be disturbed. Do not move the muscles of the face because this will cause the mask to crack and reduce its effectiveness.

Remove the mask with plenty of tepid water and cotton wool or a soft, clean face cloth.

Refresh with purified water or a toner *(see pp34-5)*, to close the pores.

Apply a thin film of moisturizer and try to leave the face bare of make-up for eight hours.

Facial facts/2

SIMPLE SECRETS

All skin types:
The infused juice of spinach and parsley mixed with oatmeal acts as a tonic mask suitable for most skins.
The juice of liquidized green peppers mixed with oatmeal makes a nourishing mask.

Dry skins:
Egg yolk mixed with honey and almond oil, or double cream mixed with honey make nutritious masks.

Dry and normal skins:
Mayonnaise by itself, or mixed with any crushed fruit or vegetable liquid or infusion, makes a nourishing and emollient mask.

Oily skins:
Beaten egg white, with or without the addition of 15ml (1 tablespoon) of skimmed milk powder, makes a tightening mask.

Sallow skins:
30ml (2 tablespoons) of household starch mixed with 15ml (1 tablespoon) of warm milk makes a bleaching, tightening mask.

REVITALIZING FRUIT MASK

A moistening protective mask, suitable for dry skins, or skins suffering from over-exposure to the sun.

½ ripe avocado
15ml (1 tbsp) fresh tomato juice
15ml (1 tbsp) fresh lemon juice

Mash the avocado flesh with the tomato and lemon juices until smooth.

YOGHURT AND YEAST MASK

A cleansing and purifying mask, suitable for all skin types.

15ml (1 tbsp) plain yoghurt
15ml (1 tbsp) brewer's yeast
5ml (1 tsp) fresh lemon juice
5ml (1 tsp) olive oil (optional – for dry skins only)

Mix all the ingredients together until smooth. This mask should not be applied before a special occasion because it activates spots, before ultimately clearing them.

BLEACHING MASK

A tightening and bleaching mask, suitable for all skin types.

30ml (2 tbsps) fuller's earth
pinch of cinnamon
pinch of bicarbonate of soda
30ml (2 tbsps) milk
5ml (1 tsp) rosewater
5ml (1 tsp) clear honey

Mix the fuller's earth, cinnamon and bicarbonate to a paste with the milk and rosewater, and add the honey.

STRAWBERRY MASK

A cleansing and healing mask, suitable for combination skins.

4 large strawberries
ground oatmeal

Mash the strawberries with enough oatmeal to make a thick paste.

OIL FACE PACK

A wonderfully effective refining mask for dry and normal mature skins. It is particularly soothing after sunbathing.

60ml (4 tbsps) fine olive oil
30ml (2 tbsps) camomile or fennel infusion (see p20)

Warm the olive oil in a bowl in a *bain-marie*. Soak enough cotton wool in it to cover your face. Place protective gauze pads over the eyes and cover your face with the olive oil compresses. Leave until cold, blot dry with tissues and follow with a warm compress of the camomile or fennel infusion. Splash your face with cold water.

ORANGE HONEY FACIAL

A refreshing and revitalizing mask, suitable for all skins and gentle enough to apply around the sensitive eye and mouth areas.

45ml (3 tbsps) clear honey
juice of ½ an orange

Warm the honey until it is fluid and add the orange juice.

NOURISHING BANANA MASK

A very nourishing mask, suitable for dry and normal skins.

250g (½ lb) ripe bananas
5ml (1 tsp) clear honey
10ml (2 tsps) thick cream
10ml (2 tsps) ground almonds

Mash and sieve, or blend the bananas with the honey, cream and almonds.

CUCUMBER MASK

A astringent and tightening mask, suitable for oily skins. Not to be used on dry and sensitive skins.

½ large peeled cucumber
2.5ml (½ tsp) fresh lemon juice
5ml (1 tsp) witch hazel
1 whisked egg white

Mash or blend the cucumber to a pulp and add the lemon juice and witch hazel. Stir in the egg white.

LECITHIN MASK

A rich and nourishing mask, suitable for dry and normal skins.

15ml (1 tbsp) lecithin
10ml (2 tsps) pure peach, apricot or apple juice
5ml (1 tsp) wheatgerm oil

Mix all ingredients together.

NECK AND THROAT MASK

A tightening and toning mask, suitable for mature skins, but not for dry or sensitive skins.

15ml (1 tbsp) milk
5ml (1 tsp) clear honey
1 egg white
5ml (1 tsp) camphor

Mix all the ingredients together and apply with a soft brush.

PROBLEMS SOLVED/1

The healing properties in the juices and pulp of fresh fruit and vegetables and in herbal compounds, together with the natural enriching, anti-bacterial properties of honey, eggs, bran and yoghurt can work to soothe a range of skin disorders. Remember, however, that all natural remedies need time to work because they gently encourage the body's own recuperative powers. If, having persevered with these remedies, the condition does not improve, seek professional advice.

PROBLEM	CAUSE	BASIC TREATMENT	HERBAL REMEDY
Acne	Hormone imbalance in adolescents, the birth pill in young women and nervous and emotional stress. The activity of the sebaceous glands is increased, causing excessive oil flow which leads to clogged and infected pores.	Beauty preparations should be chosen with this skin problem in mind. Cleansers and astringents should be mild in order to avoid further stimulation of the sebaceous glands. Ensure thorough cleansing but do not use facial steamers which may spread the infection. Face masks using natural ingredients and herbs should be used frequently.	Camomile, comfrey, elderflower, marigold, yarrow, marsh mallow, lady's mantle.
Blackheads	Overactive sebaceous glands. Oil becomes trapped in the pores by grease or dirt. Upon contact with the air this 'plug' becomes blackened. Infected blackheads cause spots or acne.	The skin should be cleansed regularly and thoroughly with a facial steamer containing healing herbs, after which it may be possible to expel the blackheads from the dilated pores by pressing the surrounding skin gently with a tissue or damp cotton wool pad. Follow with an astringent, healing mask based on yoghurt or kaolin. Dab cleansed pores with a mild herbal antiseptic.	Cucumber, comfrey, peppermint, yarrow, dandelion.
Blemished skin with rash pimples and spots	Many, varying from excessive oil secretion to allergy and infection.	Most conditions can be relieved with natural remedies. Lotions, cleansers, toners and creams should all contain herbal infusions. Healing masks containing yoghurt are effective, particularly when combined with elderflower or blackberry leaves cooked and mashed.	Raspberry, blackberry, strawberry, cucumber, garlic, onion, watercress, comfrey and parsley juices. Elderflower, marigold, lavender, rosemary, fennel, castor oil.

PROBLEM	CAUSE	BASIC TREATMENT	HERBAL REMEDY
Eczema, rashes, flaking skin	External irritants, allergies or nervous tension and emotional upsets.	Do an allergy test to find the cause, and cool the affected area with a herbal compress. Use beauty preparations for dry, sensitive skins. Calmative herbal teas will do much to alleviate this condition.	Comfrey, camomile, burdock, strawberry and blackberry leaves, potato juice.
Freckles	Melanin pigmentation in the skin; they can only be lightened.	Careful sunscreening will prevent further darkening of the pigment. Herb and fruit juice dabbed on freckles will lighten them. They can also be added to creams, lotions and yoghurt masks.	Elderflower, lime flowers, lady's mantle, cranberry, lemon juice, castor oil.
Open pores	Overactive sebaceous glands.	Pores cannot be closed, only tightened. Use frequent herbal steamers followed by a tightening mask based on oatmeal, buttermilk, clay and egg white. Use herbal astringents.	Cucumber, carrot juice, parsley, yarrow, sage, horsetail.
Scars	Acne, spots, wounds and burns.	If not too deep, scars can be made less noticeable by applying a herbal oil made with Vitamin E or wheatgerm oil.	Marigold.
Thread veins, broken or dilated veins	Skin damage, too much alcohol, pregnancy or high blood pressure.	Avoid facial steaming and hot and cold compresses. Do not use alcohol on your skin, or massage it. Use a milk cleanser. Use herbal lotions and infusions to tone down your skin colour.	Coltsfoot, yarrow, camomile, parsley, lettuce, marigold.
Warts	Not completely identified. They seem to appear and disappear for no particular reason.	They can only be removed professionally, but may be reduced if rubbed with dandelion sap.	
Wrinkles	The hardening and shrinking of collagen and elastin fibre. They can never be eradicated, except with cosmetic surgery, but can be delayed and softened.	Use fine oil particularly around the eyes and mouth. Use face masks based on buttermilk, yoghurt or honey and herbal infusions and compresses.	Camomile, chervil, lemon balsam, fennel, lime flowers, marsh mallow, marigold, elderflower.

PROBLEMS SOLVED/2

SIMPLE SECRETS

Eczema:
Grated carrot applied to the face as a mask, or carrot juice added to a lotion soothes this skin disorder. Potato juice also helps to heal eczema patches.

Spots, pimples and acne:
Herbal lotions made with the juice of liquidized parsley or comfrey are very healing if used daily. The strained liquid from simmered quince seeds is also an effective healer.

Wrinkles:
The juice from liquidized watermelon is an effective cleanser and skin softener which miraculously smoothes out wrinkles and hardened skin. Geranium (perlargonium) leaves soaked in rosewater and applied to the face help to smooth wrinkles.
Onion juice is another rather extreme (and antisocial!) skin softener.

SULPHUR MASK

An efficient deep cleansing and tightening mask which is recommended for acne sufferers. Make an allergy test (see p27) before using it, because many skins suffer an adverse reaction to sulphur.

5ml (1 tsp) sulphur powder
30ml (2 tbsps) fuller's earth
1 beaten egg white

Mix the three ingredients with enough purified water to make a smooth paste.

PLUM MASK

An astringent mask suitable for acne sufferers.

225g (8 oz) boiled plums
5ml (1 tsp) almond oil

Mash the flesh of the plums into the oil to make a thick paste.

PARSLEY LOTION

A soothing lotion which, if used daily, will help to eradicate thread veins and blotches.

13g (½ oz) fresh parsley
150ml (¼ pt) milk
3 drops tincture of benzoin

Place the parsley and the milk in a blender and mix briefly. Simmer the mixture gently in a covered pan. Leave covered until cool. Strain the mixture, pressing well. Add the benzoin, pour into a 200ml (7fl oz) bottle and keep refrigerated. Shake well before using.
   A good alternative to this lotion is made by substituting whole dark lettuce leaves for the parsley.

POTATO MASK

A very deep cleansing and healing mask for blemished and spotty skin.

15ml (1 tbsp) extracted potato juice
15ml (1 tbsp) fuller's earth

Mix the ingredients together to form a paste.

TOMATO PASTE

A healing cleanser for blackheads and clogged pores.

3-4 puréed good-sized tomatoes
fine ground oatmeal
5ml (1 tsp) clear honey

Mix the ingredients together well. Rub gently over the skin, concentrating on the worst affected areas. Leave on your skin for 10 minutes. Rinse well with tepid water.

WHITE WINE MASK

A cleansing mask, which is a very effective treatment for blackheads.

1 glass Sauternes or Rhine wine
juice of 1 lemon
30ml (2 tbsps) ground oatmeal

Mix the ingredients together to make a light paste. A white wine and lemon tonic (see p35) reinforces the effect of this mask.

ELDERFLOWER TONIC COLOGNE

Very astringent and only suitable for oily skin with enlarged pores.

60ml (4 tbsps) elderflower water (see p20)
30ml (2 tbsps) fresh cucumber juice
30ml (2 tbsps) eau de cologne
10ml (2 tsps) tincture of benzoin

Mix all the ingredients together and leave for 12 hours. Pour through a filter paper into a 150ml (¼pt) bottle. Keep refrigerated and use quickly.

ELDERFLOWER LOTION

A bleaching and softening lotion to treat freckled skins

60ml (4 tbsps) strong elderflower infusion (see p20)
15ml (1 tbsp) fresh lemon juice
2.5ml (½ tsp) alum

Mix all the ingredients together. Apply to freckles and leave for 30 minutes. Pour into a 100ml (4fl oz) bottle and keep refrigerated. Use frequently.

ELDERFLOWER AND HORSERADISH CREAM

Use this with care to treat freckles, avoiding the eye area as horseradish 'fumes' can cause stinging.

60ml (4 tbsps) sour milk
5ml (1 tsp) grated horseradish
15ml (1 tbsp) ground oatmeal

Mix the ingredients to a paste. Apply to freckles and leave for 30 minutes.

RASPBERRY MASK

A healing and cleansing mask for blemished and problem skins.

25g (1oz) raspberries
5ml (1 tsp) plain yoghurt
5ml (1 tsp) ground oatmeal

Mash the raspberries and mix them with the other ingredients to form a smooth paste.

MARIGOLD OIL

A healing oil which clears small blemishes and scars, particularly those caused by acne, burns and thread veins.

30ml (2 tbsps) fresh or 15ml (1 tbsp) dried marigold petals
60ml (4 tbsps) wheatgerm oil

Warm the oil and soak the petals in it, pounding them until they dissolve. Strain into a 100ml (4fl oz) bottle and use as necessary.

ONION MASK

An antiseptic deep cleansing mask for blemished and problem skins.

15ml (1 tbsp) liquidized onion juice
15ml (1 tbsp) kaolin
5ml (1 tsp) clear honey

Mix the ingredients together to form a smooth paste.

PEAR FACE PASTE

An antiseptic and astringent cleanser for spotty skins.

1 mashed pear
15ml (1 tbsp) powdered milk

Mix the ingredients together to form a smooth paste.

APRICOT CREAM

An excellent softening and nourishing cream, which helps to reduce wrinkles.

30ml (2 tbsps) anhydrous lanolin
15ml (1 tbsp) apricot oil
5ml (1 tsp) lemon juice
3 drops tincture of benzoin

Melt the lanolin in a bowl in a *bain-marie*. Stir in the apricot oil and lemon juice. Remove from the heat. Add the benzoin and beat continuously until cool. Pot and seal.

Healthy mouths/1

A set of fabulously arranged, identically shaped teeth is a very rare natural attribute and more often we have to make do with less than perfection. There is no reason why slightly irregular teeth should be unattractive, but since they are the first things that catch the attention when you smile and say hello, poor teeth can make a poor impression.

The only way to promote beautiful teeth is with meticulous brushing, three times a day up, down, over and around each tooth, massaging your gums well. Also, you should have regular six monthly check-ups with the dentist. Good strong teeth are formed and maintained by sticking to a well-balanced diet with a sufficient intake of proteins, calcium and vitamins. Sweet sticky foods, drinks and snacks should be avoided. Instead, eat plenty of raw crunchy fruit and vegetables to encourage healthy teeth and gums.

Dental decay and gum disease are caused by plaque bacteria that combine with any residual sugar in the mouth to form acid. This acid not only causes decay, but also penetrates the gums causing inflammation, bleeding and disease, which can lead to the loss of teeth.

There is nothing more attractive than a fresh, healthy mouth. Keep your teeth in tip-top condition and your lips well protected with pure, natural products.

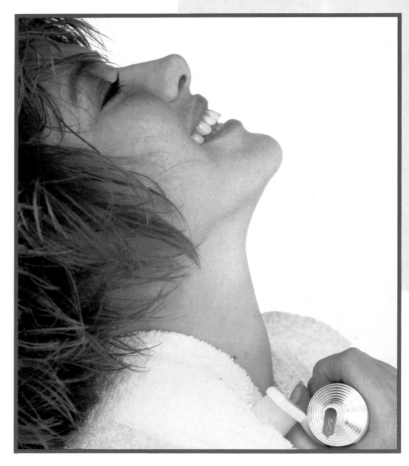

How to ensure oral hygiene

Methods of cleaning teeth vary from painstaking massage with well chewed pieces of bark or stripped twigs, to sophisticated fluoride toothpastes and electric toothbrushes. It is, however, the time taken over tooth care that is the really important factor, not the method or products involved.

Many people are strongly opposed to the abrasives and detergents found in commercial toothpastes and consider them to do more harm than good. The ingredients used in natural toothpaste and mouthwashes will cleanse, remove stains and deodorize more gently and just as efficiently. If your local water supply lacks fluoride and you feel it is necessary, use a fluoride tablet when rinsing your mouth after cleaning your teeth.

Keep your lips smooth and supple and protect them from splits and tears which are not only painful and debilitating but can lead to infections.

Healthy mouths/2

SIMPLE SECRETS
Simple gargles:
Lavender or rosewater, mild infusions of aniseed, thyme, peppermint, marjoram.

Breath fresheners:
Chewed mint, parsley, watercress, cloves.

Cleansers to rub on teeth:
Sage leaves, strawberries, lemon peel, apple juice.

LEMON PEEL POWDER

An excellent stain remover.

30ml (2 tbsps) ground dried lemon peel
30ml (2 tbsps) bicarbonate of soda
30ml (2 tbsps) fine sea salt

Mix the ingredients together. Pot and seal tightly – all powders must be kept in airtight containers.

SAGE AND SALT POWDER

An antiseptic and efficient cleanser.

30ml (2 tbsps) fine sea salt
30ml (2 tbsps) dried sage

Pound the ingredients together and warm in the oven on a china dish until they become blackened. Pound once again. Pot and seal.

CINNAMON POWDER FOR SENSITIVE TEETH

A gentle cleanser.

30ml (2 tbsps) ground cinnamon
60ml (4 tbsps) arrowroot

Mix the ingredients well together and store in an airtight container. Mix a little of the powder to a paste with water to use.

SALT RINSE

An effective antiseptic mouth rinse which heals bleeding gums.

10ml (2 tsps) sea salt
2 drops of 10 vol. peroxide

Mix the two ingredients in a glass of water and swill around the mouth and gums before spitting out.

MINT AND ROSEMARY MOUTHWASH

A pleasantly antiseptic rinse.

5ml (1 tsp) fresh or 2.5ml (½ tsp) dried mint
5ml (1 tsp) fresh or 2.5ml (½ tsp) dried rosemary
575ml (1pt) purified water
2.5ml (½ tsp) tincture of myrrh

Boil the water and make an infusion with the herbs (see p20). Allow the infusion to cool. Filter it and add the myrrh. Keep refrigerated.

EUCALYPTUS MOUTHWASH

A freshening rinse incorporating oil of cloves and myrrh, which are frequently used to sooth sore gums.

13g (½ oz) dried eucalyptus leaves
700ml (1¼ pt) purified water
2 drops oil of cloves
2 drops tincture of myrrh

Simmer the leaves in the water for seven minutes. Cover tightly and leave overnight. Strain and add the clove and myrrh oils to the liquid. Shake well and keep refrigerated.

BASIC LIP SALVE

This should be used as an everyday protective cream.

10ml (2 tsps) beeswax
20ml (4 tsps) almond oil
5ml (1 tsp) rosewater

Melt the beeswax in a bowl in a *bain-marie* and beat in the oil. Remove from the heat and stir in the rosewater, having first warmed it in a separate bowl. Pot while it is still warm.

LIP GLOSS

Use this for soft, shiny protected lips.

2.5ml (½ tsp) beeswax
30ml (2 tbsps) cocoa butter

Melt the ingredients together in a bowl in a *bain-marie* and pot while warm.

LIP PROTECTOR

A soothing lip salve to stop your lips drying out in the sun.

45ml (3 tbsps) beeswax
15ml (1 tbsp) clear honey
45ml (3 tbsps) sesame oil

Melt the beeswax in a bowl in a *bain-marie* and add the honey. Beat in the oil. Pour the mixture into a small pot.

EYEBRIGHT

Your eyes reflect your state of mind and health to an extraordinary degree. Lack of sleep, too much alcohol, too many cigarettes, air conditioning, central heating, wind, weather and stress all have a severe effect on your eyes. Steps must be taken to preserve the health and beauty of these precious assets, so begin by treating them from within.

Drink plenty of water to purify your system; eat plenty of fresh, raw vegetables, especially carrots, rich in Vitamin A, which is renowned for its regenerative effect on eyes strained by harsh lighting; and make sure you have enough sleep and take adequate exercise.

Your eyes are very efficient self-healers, producing tears to deal with localized irritations, but at times they need a little extra help. When they are tired, bloodshot and prickly, they should be soothed with a herbal eyebath or compress which will also reduce any puffiness or surrounding shadows.

The skin around your eyes is extremely delicate and requires special care. Only the finest oils, such as apricot or almond, should be used to treat this area. Gently massage oil around your eyes to reduce wrinkling and remove eye make-up. Cotton wool pads soaked in a warm oil and laid on the eyes while you take a rest help to keep the skin supple and free of lines. Make sure that the skin is not dragged when applying or removing make-up and is never subjected to heavy cosmetic creams. Avocado and almond cream *(see p36)* and nourishing Marigold and Wheatgerm cream *(see p37)* are light, easily absorbed creams suitable for the eye area. Face masks should never be applied around the eyes, unless the recipe specifically allows for this, as is the case with the Orange Honey Facial mask *(see p45)*.

Finally, remember that your eyes reflect your mood, so think and behave with positive enthusiasm to promote an attractive sparkle in your eyes.

SIMPLE SECRETS
Tired eyes:
To relieve tension in tired eyes, press the base of the palms of the hands over closed eyelids and maintain the pressure for several minutes. Using a little fine oil and the tips of three of your fingers stroke gently from the bridge of the nose out across the eyes to the temple several times.
Thin slices of cucumber placed over the eyes are cooling and refreshing.
Herbal compresses made with any of the following infusions are soothing, healing and relaxing: rosemary, sage, elderflower, cornflower, verbena, angelica, fennel, borage, camomile, goldenseal and coltsfoot.

Under-eye puffiness:
Place wafer thin slices of potato over your closed eyes, or apply a piece of gauze covered with grated apple or potato. Warm tea bags, particularly rosehip, camomile and papaya, laid on the eyes are also effective.

Dark shadows:
The juice from crushed mint reduces dark shadows.

Sparse lashes and brows:
Castor oil stimulates the growth of eyelashes, while olive oil improves the condition of sparse eyebrows.

NASTURTIUM SEED COMPRESS

An antiseptic and soothing treatment for styes.

15ml (1 tbsp) nasturtium seeds
15ml (1 tbsp) raw grated potato

Blend the ingredients together and place them on a piece of gauze. Lay on the eyes, gauze side down.

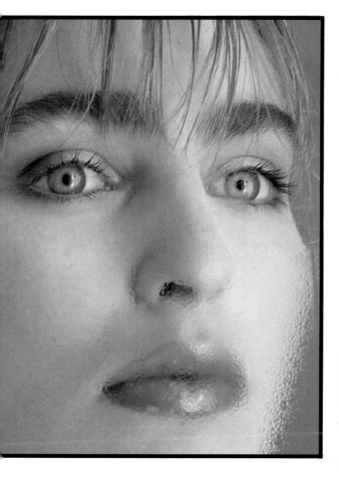

A pair of beautiful, clear eyes illuminates a face. Your eyes are exceptionally delicate and require the gentlest of cosmetic care, a sensible diet and plenty of sleep if they are to look their best.

MARIGOLD AND APPLE

A soothing refresher for tired eyes.

90ml (6 tbsps) strong marigold infusion (see p20)
1 peeled grated apple

Mix the ingredients together and stew gently until soft. When cooled apply as above.

EYEBRIGHT LOTION

Herbal eyebaths soothe and refresh tired eyes. Eyebright, as its name suggests, is the perfect herb to use in eye lotions.

60ml (4 tbsps) fresh or 30ml (2 tbsps) dried eyebright
275ml (½pt) boiling water

Infuse the herbs in the water until the liquid cools. Strain several times through filter paper and bottle. Use whenever necessary.

LECITHIN EYE CREAM

A fine oily protein enriched cream that is easily absorbed into delicate skin.

15ml (1 tbsp) anhydrous lanolin
22.5ml (1½ tbsps) almond oil
5ml (1 tsp) powdered lecithin
10ml (2 tsps) purified water

Melt the lanolin in a bowl in a *bain-marie* and add the almond oil. Remove from the heat and stir in the lecithin until smooth. Warm the water and add it to this mixture, beating constantly. Pot and seal.

OILY EYE MAKE-UP REMOVER

A very gentle combination of oils.

30ml (2 tbsps) almond oil
15ml (1 tbsp) castor oil

Shake the oils together in a bottle until well combined. Use on a cotton wool pad to remove make-up, taking care not to stretch the skin. You should wipe make-up off with a circular sweeping action moving from the upper inner corner of your eyelid around the outer corner to finish by your nose.

CROWNING GLORY

A head of shining hair that gleams with health and life is every woman's ideal. Using hair care products made from natural ingredients guarantees gentle and therapeutic treatment.

CROWNING GLORY

The type of hair you are born with cannot be changed, but it is within your power to improve upon its natural state. If you cannot alter the number of hairs on your head, their growth rate or texture you can certainly ensure that your hair is always at the peak of condition and health. With a thorough understanding of your hair comes the ability to deal with its problems and highlight its good qualities.

Hair facts

The visible part of the hair is the hair shaft, which is made up of three layers – the hard outer layer or cuticle of *keratin* scales, the inner cortex of protein fibres and the centre medulla that contains a substance similar to bone marrow and is attached directly to the hair root in the follicle.

The outer layer of keratin scales should lie flat so that hair looks smooth and shiny, but if they are damaged they will be ruffled resulting in hair that looks fluffy, dull and dry. The inner cortex determines the strength, elasticity and colour of the hair and when it becomes brittle the hair will break.

At the base of the hair follicle is the papilla, which nourishes the growing hair from its root to the point where it leaves the scalp. Near the surface of the skin, the sebaceous gland feeds the emerging hair with oil or sebum. Once the hair leaves the scalp it is in effect dead matter.

There are on average 100,000 strands of hair on every head. The variance in number is associated with hair colour and fineness, blondes having more hairs on their heads than brunettes.

How to care for your hair

The condition of your hair depends entirely on the way you treat it. You must nourish it from within with an adequate intake of proteins and Vitamin B, which is particularly vital for good hair condition, a well-balanced diet and plenty of water. Your hair always reacts to fluctuations in your overall body condition and will appear lacklustre after illness, childbirth or any intense stress or shock. At such times your body is using up all its resources to meet the demands put upon it and you should supplement your diet to maintain the correct balance of necessary nutrients.

Once hair has been externally damaged there is little that you can do except treat it with the appropriate shampoos and conditioners, and massage and feed the scalp. No amount of conditioner can regenerate split and dehydrated hair. Trim away any split ends and wait for the natural regenerative processes to repair the damage.

Assessing your hair type

You cannot expect to achieve the best results from your hair until you are thoroughly at home with all its shortcomings and advantages. You can use the chart overleaf for an instant appraisal of your hair type and its inherent problems. Once you have recognized any problem relevant to your hair you can overcome it and regain confidence in your appearance. Improvement requires specific treatment – the correct shampoos, rinses and conditioners used with care and thought to complement each other.

It is not enough, however, just to understand your hair type. You must also make yourself aware of its tendencies regarding its growth rate, colour and texture before you choose a new style or treatment. Changing you hair style or colour can be a wonderful tonic, but several factors must be taken into consideration – the shape of your face, your height and shape and your skin and eye colour. You should also consider whether your hair grows too slowly to compensate for what could be a drastically short haircut and whether the style you fancy would fit in with your lifestyle. It is also true that certain hairstyles suit some hair types better than others, so do not undo all your hard conditioning work by choosing unwisely.

Hair care/1

HAIR HERBS AND HAIR TYPES

Use this short list of herbs *(see below)* to choose the herbal remedy suitable to your hair type. You can choose from the wide range of natural rinses the particular herbal treatment that will most benefit the condition of your hair and your scalp with the help of the easy-to-follow hair type chart *(see right)*. The suitable herbs should be incorporated in all your hair care products for the best results.

Natural Power

Burdock root:	prevents dandruff
Camomile:	lightens, softens
Catmint:	soothes scalp conditions, promotes growth
Cloves:	highlight dark hair
Comfrey:	heals scalp problems
Elderflower:	lightens and conditions blonde and greying hair
Goosegrass (Cleavers):	prevents dandruff
Ginger root:	light colouring agent for red hair
Henna:	powerful red colourant
Lavender:	tones and conditions oily hair
Lemon verbena:	improves sheen and highlights dark hair
Lime flowers:	soften and condition
Marigold:	golden red hair rinse
Marjoram (Oregano):	prevents dandruff promotes hair growth
Mullein:	gold lightener
Nasturtium:	promotes growth
Parsley:	improves hair colour and shine, prevents dandruff
Privet:	darkens hair
Quince seeds:	prevent dandruff
Raspberry leaves:	improve scalp condition, soften hair
Red oak bark:	dark red colourant
Rosemary:	tones, conditions, prevents dandruff, darkens hair
Rhubarb root and stem:	effective gold hair lightener
Saffron:	golden red colour
Sage:	conditions and colours dark and grey hair
Soapwort:	cleanses
Southernwood:	prevents dandruff promotes hair growth
Thyme:	antiseptic, conditions
Walnut leaves and shells:	strong darkening rinse
Witch hazel:	astringent, cleanses oily hair
Yarrow:	antiseptic, cleanses oily hair

DESCRIPTION

OILY HAIR

Oily hair is typically thin, lank, requires frequent washing and quickly becomes limp and lifeless. It is also associated with an oily skin and dandruff, and is often accompanied by odour. It does not respond easily to styling but reacts well to light perming, colouring and bleaching, because the drying action of the chemicals fights the greasiness

DRY HAIR

Dry hair is usually recognized as being dull and brittle, splitting easily and often is accompanied by a dry flaking scalp caused by sluggish oil production at the base of the hair shafts. Dry fragile hair like this is hereditary and comes with a dry skin. Dry hair can be caused by perming and commercial hair colorants, overexposure to the elements, salt and chlorinated water. Protect dry hair at all times.

AGEING HAIR

From the age of 30, nourishment to the hair follicle begins to slow down. Gradually the ageing process causes any previous problems to become exaggerated and introduces new ones such lack of life, colour and lustre and the appearance of grey hairs.

MIXED CONDITION HAIR

Hair condition can become problematic when the oil from the sebaceous glands soaks into dried skin cells on the scalp, clogging the follicle and preventing an even flow of oil along the hair shaft. The scalp becomes oily and itchy, while the hair is dry and unmanageable. This combination of problems must be cured at their source and then controlled to prevent a recurrence.

PROBLEM HAIR

It is dandruff which normally characterizes problem hair. This scaly condition of the scalp is caused by the hair follicle becoming blocked by excess sebum. This can be caused by stress and emotional strain. It can also be caused by keeping hair covered.

SHAMPOO	CONDITIONING	RINSING	STYLING
...ash daily with a mild shampoo, ...oiding commercial anti-...ndruff and 'drying' shampoos ...cause these strip the hair shaft ...oil without getting at the ...urce of the problem. Lather ...ntly using warm water, taking ...re not to scrub or massage the ...alp and thereby overstimulate ...e sebaceous glands. Rinse very ...ell.	A conditioner is not often required. Once a week cleanse the scalp, after shampooing, with a cotton wool pad soaked in a mild natural astringent, working down partings in the hair until the entire head has been treated.	Rinse well with plenty of cool water adding a herbal rinse or mild astringent in the final rinse to reduce oiliness and add sheen.	Avoid greasy lotions or gels, using only those with an alcohol or astringent base to give body to flyaway hair. Do not brush vigorously, or use heated appliances, such as curling tongs or hot brushes, or direct heat, as this stimulates the oil flow.
...ash twice a week using a very ...ld or enriched shampoo and ...arm water. Massage the scalp ...ntly to stimulate the sebaceous ...ands.	Dry hair always requires an enriching conditioner, either of the pre-shampoo variety or after every wash. An additional overnight oil treatment once a month is very beneficial. Gentle herbal hair colorants also condition by coating the hair shaft and giving hair body without chemical abuse.	Use cool water and a mild herbal rinse to enhance hair colour and shine.	Do not comb or rub wet hair, but wrap it in a towel. Avoid alcohol-based gels and lotions which will exacerbate the scalp condition and dry the ends of the hair. Avoid direct heat or heated appliances and allow hair to dry naturally, if possible, using a wide-toothed comb when dry. Use rag rollers to curl.
...ash regularly with a very mild ...ampoo in lukewarm water. ...assage the scalp gently to ...prove circulation, thereby ...ducing the risk of dandruff, ...hich can unexpectedly occur.	Use a nourishing instant conditioner suited to your hair type after every shampoo and apply a deep treatment conditioner once a week. A mild, discreet herbal colorant will give body and lustre while protecting the hair shaft from damage.	Rinse with cool water and a herbal rinse, or add vinegar or lemon juice to the finishing rinse to restore the acid balance and sheen.	Use gentle heat to dry, avoiding heated appliances. Do not brush vigorously; use a wide-toothed comb to style it. Use rag rollers to curl.
...order to clear the scalp of ...kes of dry skin, soak it ...roughly in a bowl of tepid ...ter with one tablespoon of ...er vinegar and use a mild anti-...ndruff shampoo every other ...y until the condition clears. ...en shampoo as for dry hair.	Use a light conditioner for normal hair.	Use an anti-dandruff lotion or mild astringent to keep the scalp free of flaking scales.	Dry naturally and use only a natural thickening gel to give body without disturbing hair condition.
...st rinse the scalp thoroughly in ...owl of water with one ...blespoon of cider vinegar. ...ampoo daily in lukewarm ...ater using a mild baby shampoo ...th added anti-dandruff ...operties. The scalp must be ...pt scrupulously clean but do ...t scrub or massage hard.	Gently massage morning and evening with a herbal anti-dandruff lotion, or use an anti-dandruff conditioner two or three times a week after shampooing. The use of herbs and natural products is of particular value in the treatment of dandruff, as they are mild and cannot damage the hair or scalp.	Rinse very thoroughly using a herbal or lemon rinse.	Make sure that your brushes and combs are immaculately clean every time you use them. Do not brush your hair vigorously or use gels and setting lotions until the condition is completely cleared. Do not heat directly or use heated appliances.

To make a strand test:
It is absolutely essential to test the reaction of your hair to a herbal colorant before you use it. It is the only way to be certain of the final effect. Snip off a small lock of hair and apply the dye to it *(see below)*.

HERBAL BRILLIANCE

There is a strong case for the use of natural products in hair care, because they act only very gently to protect and improve the hair. Commercial hair care products contain everything from detergents to harsh chemicals that can cause damage. They are also an unnecessary expense considering that the ingredients for hair rinses and conditioners are readily at hand in most kitchens.

Herbal colour rinses and more permanent colcrants are on the whole very subtle. They also strengthen and condition the hair, by encasing each hair shaft with colour, instead of chemically attacking its structure. Eventually the colour will fade, rather than grow out, so if you make a mistake you can gain comfort from the knowledge that it need not last long.

ALLERGIES AND STRAND TESTS

However kind and gentle natural products are to our hair and skin, some people will be allergic to them. This is particularly likely when using colorants, so you should make an allergy reaction patch test *(see p27)* before you use any colorant.

The effect of a colourant on your hair can only be judged by making a strand test. This is particularly important if your hair has been treated with chemical colorants, permed, exposed to sun, sea, wind or chlorine, or if you have been in poor health, because it will be especially porous and brittle. Hair in this condition can react badly when treated with a herbal tint.

To make an effective test, snip off a small piece of hair and apply the colorant you want to try to it. Leave it for the specified time, rinse it and check to see whether your hair has responded well. In this way you can see exactly how long you should leave the colorant on to achieve the desired shade and whether that shade suits you.

SHAMPOOS

A normal healthy head of hair requires frequent washing so it is essential that you use the correct shampoo. It should be mild, to ensure that the hair shaft is not stripped of natural oils, and colour-enhancing. When washing your hair, use warm water, never hot, which not only overstimulates the sebaceous glands, but is also detrimental to the hair shaft. Spread a little shampoo between your palms and gently massage evenly through your hair. Unless your hair is very dirty it should not need more than one application of shampoo. Rinse well using warm, then cool water.

Dry shampoos are efficient and easily made cleansers for use between washes to give your hair a lift.

Keep your hair looking and feeling lustrous and healthy with natural, mild shampoos, conditioners and rinses.

Hair care/3

SIMPLE HERBAL SHAMPOO

Any of the herbs listed on *p60* can be used to remedy specific problems in the gentlest of shampoos.

45ml (3 tbsps) strong herbal infusion (see p20)
10ml (2 tsps) mild baby shampoo

Whisk the ingredients together.

A PURE SOAP BASE FOR SHAMPOO

This can be added to a strong herbal infusion in quantities of two tablespoons of each.

100g (4oz) pure Castile or olive oil soap
575ml (1pt) warm water

Grate the soap and put it in a large 850ml (1½pt) glass jar with the water. Cover and leave for two to three days in a warm place shaking and stirring frequently.

EGG AND BRANDY SHAMPOO

A good all-purpose conditioning shampoo.

75ml (⅛pt) brandy
75ml (⅛pt) warm water
2 egg yolks

Combine the liquids and slowly beat in the egg yolks. Use at once, massaging gently into the hair and leave for 10 minutes. Rinse well in warm water.

EGG SHAMPOOS

Eggs make natural enriching shampoos. Remember not to use them with hot water as the egg will harden.

All hair types:
2 eggs whisked into 150ml (¼pt) warm water.
Normal and dry hair:
1 egg whisked into 30ml (2 tbsps) baby shampoo.
Dry hair:
1 egg yolk whisked into 150ml (¼pt) warm herbal infusion (see p20).
Oily hair:
1 egg white whisked into 150ml (¼pt) warm herbal infusion (see p20).

Leave all shampoos on the hair for 5-10 minutes before rinsing.

ORRIS ROOT DRY SHAMPOO

Suitable for normal hair.

30ml (2 tbsps) orris root
30ml (2 tbsps) arrowroot

Mix the ingredients together. Part the hair in sections all over the head, sprinkling the powder along the roots as you go. Rub in gently and leave for 30 minutes. Brush vigorously with a bristle brush to remove all traces of dirt.

FLOWER WATER CLEANSER

Suitable for normal and oily hair.
Cover a bristle brush with an old clean nylon stocking. Sprinkle with lavender water or eau de cologne and brush your hair well until it is fresh and shining. A soft bristle brush sprinkled with rosewater is a more effective treatment for dry hair.

CONDITIONERS

Hair conditioners work in much the same way as conditioners for the skin, replacing natural oils which flow from the hair follicle down the hair shaft lubricating and protecting it. Hair that has been abused with harsh treatments has been stripped of its natural oil, becoming brittle and dry and prone to split ends. Long hair often suffers more in this respect than short hair because the sebum produced at the follicle does not travel all the way down the hair shaft. Instant conditioners used after every shampoo encase the hair shaft in waxy substances ensuring protection from further damage by making it easier to comb and giving it bounce and lustre.

Deep treatment conditioners, used prior to shampooing, work at the root of the hair to feed and stimulate the hair follicle. These are usually applied once a week for problem hair and once a month for generally maintaining a beautiful head of hair. They should be massaged gently into the scalp and left under hot towels for a minimum of one hour or, to ensure penetration, overnight.

Most hair types benefit from regular conditioning, but oily hair only needs treatment when a specific problem arises. To gain the best effects from your chosen conditioner, massage it into your hair in the following way:

Apply the conditioner when your hair is wet. Start at the back of your head, using the pads of your fingertips and press firmly against your scalp. Work from the back to the front of the head using small circular motions which actually move the skin on your scalp, encouraging good circulation and easing tension.

SIMPLE SECRETS

Irritated scalp:
Oil of nettle massaged regularly into the scalp soothes irritation.
Olive oil infused with rosemary or catmint strengthens dark hair and alleviates an itchy scalp.

Over-fine hair:
Sunflower oil infused with parsley seed, marsh mallow or southernwood strengthens fair hair.

AVOCADO INSTANT CONDITIONER

Gives body to flyaway hair.

½ ripe avocado
5ml (1 tsp) avocado oil
1 egg yolk

Pulp the avocado flesh and whisk in the oil and egg yolk. Massage into the shampooed hair and leave for five minutes. Rinse thoroughly with warm water.
    Mashed avocado added to home-made mayonnaise is an excellent conditioner, as is mayonnaise alone.

YOGHURT AND EGG CONDITIONER

Good for oily and mixed condition hair that tends to be uncontrollable after washing.

150ml (¼pt) natural yoghurt
1 egg

Whisk the ingredients together and massage into the hair after shampooing. Leave for five minutes. Rinse thoroughly with warm water.

PROTEIN OIL CONDITIONER

A superb conditioner for dry hair. Use the herb oil suited to your hair type.

45ml (3 tbsps) herbal oil (see p21)
15ml (1 tbsp) cider vinegar
1 egg (yolk only for dry hair)
5ml (1 tsp) clear honey

Warm the oil in a bowl in a *bain-marie* with the honey. Beat the vinegar and egg together. Remove the oil from the heat and slowly add to the vinegar and egg mixture. Apply as for the Oil Pre-Conditioner *(see p73)*, but leave for only one hour.

HAIR CARE/4

COCONUT OIL CONDITIONER

Gives bounce and body.

30ml (2 tbsps) coconut oil
15ml (1 tbsp) cider or herbal vinegar (see p21)
1 egg

Melt the coconut oil in a bowl in a *bain-marie*. Whisk the vinegar and egg together and add slowly to the warm oil, beating continuously. Use immediately while still warm. Apply as for the Oil Pre-conditioner *(see p73)*, but leave for only three hours.

AVOCADO CONDITIONER

Promotes growth in dull lifeless and thinning hair.

30ml (2 tbsps) avocado oil
15ml (1 tbsp) castor oil
1 egg yolk

Combine the oils with the egg and apply as for the Oil Pre-conditioner *(see p73)*, but leave for only 30 minutes.

ROSEMARY AND CASTOR OIL CONDITIONER

A very healing conditioner for hair left dull and lifeless after illness.

30ml (2 tbsps) castor oil
4 drops oil of rosemary

Warm the castor oil in a bowl in a *bain-marie* and add the oil of rosemary. Massage into the hair while it is still warm. Cover your head and leave overnight. Wash out with a mild shampoo.

SOUTHERNWOOD TONIC

Promotes growth in thin hair.

75ml (5 tbsps) strong southernwood infusion (see p20)
75ml (5 tbsps) mild eau de cologne

Pour the ingredients into a 200ml (7fl oz) bottle and shake well. Use diluted with warm water – one tablespoon of each – and massage into the scalp twice a week.

RUM AND ONION TONIC

An effective, rather anti-social treatment for falling hair.

1 medium sized onion
white or dark rum

Steep the sliced, not peeled, onion in enough rum to cover it completely. Leave for 24 hours then strain. Massage a little into the scalp each night until the condition improves and then once a week until hair loss is reduced.

APPLE JUICE TONIC

Clears dandruff.

15ml (1 tbsp) pure apple juice
45ml (3 tbsps) warm water

Mix the ingredients together in a small bottle and massage into the scalp 2-3 times a week.

ROSEMARY AND BORAX

Clears dandruff.

75ml (5 tbsps) strong rosemary infusion (see p20)
pinch of borax

Mix the ingredients together and massage into the scalp daily.

RINSING

Rinsing the hair with plenty of fresh water until it is squeaky clean is the most essential stage of the hair care routine. A final rinse removes the last traces of soap and can become an important beneficial treatment if a conditioning ingredient is added to it. A thorough rinse, as cold as you can stand it, will replace the acid mantle of the hair and tighten the tiny keratin scales on the outer layer of the hair shaft, leaving your hair with a silky sheen.

The most commonly used rinses are cider vinegar and lemon juice – for dark and blonde hair respectively. Rose, lavender and orange flower waters and eau de cologne will have a mildly tonic effect on the hair.

Following the information on the Hair Herbs chart *(see p60)* you can choose which herbs to make rinses from, according to your requirements. Make up 575ml (1pint) of strong herbal infusion *(see p20)*. When it is cold, strain it through a filter paper to ensure that it is completely clear before using on your hair. Herbal rinses like these stimulate hair growth and help to alleviate scalp problems.

LIGHT CHESTNUT RINSE

Adds highlights to brown hair.

50g (2oz) privet leaves
575ml (1pt) boiling water
10ml (2 tsps) quince juice

Infuse the privet leaves in the water overnight. Stir in the quince juice. Strain the liquid through filter paper and add to the final rinsing water.

RHUBARB RINSE

Adds reddish gold highlights to brown and mousy hair.
NB: NEVER use an aluminium pan to simmer the rhubarb root solution – the reaction will form a poisonous acidic substance.

60ml (4 tbsps) ground rhubarb root
850ml (1½ pts) water

Using a stainless steel or enamel pan, simmer the powder in the water for 30 minutes. Remove from the heat, cover and leave to cool. Strain through filter paper before adding to the final rinsing water.

ASHY RINSE

Darkens ginger hair.

575ml (1pt) strong Indian tea
45ml (3 tbsps) dark rum

Leave the tea to stand until it is cold. Strain and add to the rum. Comb the mixture through your hair daily.

Styling Hair

DRYING AND STYLING HAIR

It is all too easy to undo the benefits your hair has gained from careful shampooing, conditioning and rinsing when you come to style it. After rinsing, squeeze the excess water gently from your hair between the palms of your hands.

Blot your hair dry with a clean towel and then comb it gently with a wide-toothed comb, starting from the ends and working up gradually to the scalp, taking care not to pull at any tangles. Hair should not be subjected to direct heat or heated appliances regularly. This will make dry hair very brittle and will increase the flow of oil and exacerbate the scalp condition of oily hair. Blow dry to style only when your hair is nearly dry, and then at a very gentle heat.

Setting hair on rollers should be done when the hair is nearly dry to avoid tightening or breaking of the hair shaft. The best and most comfortable method is to use old-fashioned rag rollers.

There are differing opinions on the subject of brushing. Some types of hair benefit from vigorous brushing with a good bristle brush, but other types should be styled with a comb or a brush with widely-spaced soft plastic bristles. Whichever method you use, make sure that you keep any equipment immaculately clean.

Only use setting lotions and after-styling conditioners that are gentle and give bounce and lustre to your hair. Although hair spray is considered necessary by many stylists, your hair should ideally be in good enough condition to hold its shape without the use of this rather harsh substance.

SIMPLE SECRETS
All hair types:
Beer – gives bounce, body and makes setting your hair easy.
Gelatine – 30ml (2 tablespoons) whisked into 275ml (½ pint) of boiling water and used as a final rinse.
Sugar – 15ml (1 tablespoon) dissolved in 150ml (¼ pint) of boiling water. Rag rollers and sugar water were the Victorian recipe for perfect ringlets.

Oily hair
Lemon juice – gives a very firm hold and shine.

Hair spray
Lemon juice and sugar, or sugar water alone, can be decanted into an atomiser and used as a light spray.
Long straight hair can be controlled and conditioned by brushing in several drops of oil of rosemary on a soft bristle brush. If you have dry hair, you could use any suitable herbal or aromatic oil in the same way.

You can achieve a variety of modern hairstyles using natural setting lotions and gels, from the excitingly glamorous *(above)*, to the softly natural *(above right)*.

NATURAL COLOUR

Giving your hair a colour change can be a great morale booster, but chemical colorants can damage the hair by stripping it of its natural oils. Natural hair colorants give colour, body and lustre safely, but it is still wise to take precautions to ensure reliable and flattering results.

Most natural hair colorants build up colour gradually with each application. Stronger dyes, however, have an instant effect. Rhubarb dye brightens and lightens all shades of brown hair on its first application, and the colour intensifies with progressive treatments. Henna, the strongest of the dyes, should be used carefully and only on dark and red hair. It can create a range of beautiful shades ranging from reddish gold to a gorgeous rich auburn, but if used on blonde or grey hair, it produces effects ranging from the flamboyant to the brassy.

Because the effect of natural dyes is unpredictable, it is essential to make a strand test *(see p62)* so that the nature of your hair in terms of its receptivity to the dye can be gauged.

Natural herbal hair colorants bring a range of subtle lights to your hair ranging from golden highlights, to warm reddish tones *(right)*, to dark dusky shades.

APPLYING HAIR DYES

- Use rubber gloves before applying colour as some dyes, particularly henna, stain the skin.

- Mark off a section of hair at a time with a comb.

- Using a 12mm (½in) paintbrush, apply a good quantity of dye to the roots.

- Cover your head with a plastic shower cap and swathe it in a hot towel.

- Leave for the required time.

- Rinse and wash thoroughly with a mild shampoo. Finish with a conditioning rinse.

BASIC HENNA DYE

Henna is a conditioning herb, but it is also astringent and the following recipe is the most successful method of ensuring a good colour with additional conditioning and strengthening properties. Henna should not be used on chemically treated or grey hair.

To change the shades of henna substitute one of the following liquids for the water:
  Strong camomile infusion: light golden red
  Strong black tea: subtle cool shade
  Strong tea: bright highlights
  Strong beetroot decoction: plum red for dark hair
  Strong sage infusion: subtle darker highlights

100g (4oz) henna powder
150ml (¼ pt) water
1 beaten egg
5ml (1 tbsp) castor oil

Apply to the hair, cover and leave for 15 minutes to one hour, depending on the brightness of the colour desired. Rinse well. Rub a little oil through the hair to counteract the astringent properties of the rhubarb. Wait for five minutes before shampooing.

WALNUT PASTE

This gives lustrous deep tones to dark hair. The infusion made when walnut shells and leaves are boiled in water for several hours and then strained makes a very effective hair rinse which deepens hair colour.

90ml (6 tbsps) finely ground green walnut skins
30ml (2 tbsps) powdered alum
orange flower water

Mix the ground walnut skins and alum together with enough orange flower water to make a firm paste. Apply and leave for 15 minutes to one hour depending on the intensity of shade desired.

DARK HAIR RINSE

A darkening and conditioning rinse, suitable for dark and grey hair.

30ml (2 tbsps) fresh or 15ml (1 tbsp) dried sage
*   leaves*
30ml (2 tbsps) fresh or 15ml (1 tbsp) dried
*   rosemary*
575ml (1 pt) strong Indian tea

Infuse the herbs in the boiled tea until it cools. Strain through filter paper and comb through the hair daily.

FAIR HAIR RINSE

A conditioning highlighter for fair and mousy hair.

30ml (2 tbsps) fresh or 15ml (1 tbsp) dried
*   camomile flowers*
30ml (2 tbsps) fresh or 15ml (1 tbsp) dried
*   marigold flowers*
or:
60ml (4 tbsps) fresh or 30ml (2 tbsps) dried
*   camomile flowers*
575ml (1pt) water
30ml (2 tbsps) fresh lemon juice

Infuse the flowers in the boiling water until it cools. Add the lemon juice. Strain through filter paper and add to your final rinse.

Both these rinses can be intensified and made into very effective and permanent dyes by adding enough kaolin to the strained liquid to make a fairly firm paste. Apply to your hair and leave for 15 minutes to one hour. Many highlighting herbs can be used in this way.

Mix the powder and water together in a bowl and place in a *bain-marie*. Bring to the boil and add the egg and oil. Make sure that the mixture is smooth and kept hot during application. Cover your head with a plastic shower cap and swathe in a hot towel. Leave for 15 minutes to three hours or more, depending on the depth of colour desired, which can range from subtle highlights to a vivid red. Rinse, shampoo and finish with a cool conditioning rinse.

BASIC RHUBARB DYE

This dye lightens at once but needs several applications to give the hair a rich reddish gold colour. It is especially effective on brown and mousy hair.

275ml (½ pt) strong decoction of rhubarb stem
*   and root (see p20)*
Kaolin powder
1 egg yolk
Castor oil

Warm the decoction in a bowl in a *bain-marie*. Mix it with the egg yolk and enough kaolin to form a paste.

PROBLEMS SOLVED/3

	CAUSE	TREATMENT	HERBAL REMEDY
HAIR LOSS, THINNING AND LIFELESS HAIR	Excessive hair loss can be caused by anxiety, tension and hormonal upsets, drugs and illness.	First pinpoint the cause of the problem. If it is curable, embark on a high protein fresh fruit and vegetable diet, supplemented by brewer's yeast tablets. Use a mild herbal shampoo and rinse daily, and a protein or oil-based conditioner well massaged into the scalp. A restorative tonic should be rubbed in daily. Dry hair naturally and brush carefully with a soft bristle brush. If the condition persists consult a trichologist.	Onion, garlic, chilli, quince, castor oil and rum. Oil of cedarwood and southernwood. Infusions of mallow root, parsley seed, rosemary, catmint, nasturtium and marjoram (oregano).
BREAKING HAIR AND SPLIT ENDS	External abuse, colouring, bleaching, perming, chlorine and overexposure to the elements all lead to this condition.	Have the ends trimmed regularly. Avoid astringent lotions. Use a protein enriched shampoo. Condition after each shampoo and use a deep treatment oil conditioner once a week. Do not brush your hair, use only a wide-toothed comb. Do not use heated appliances or direct heat.	
DANDRUFF	A scaly condition of the scalp is often associated with an oily skin and acne, but is as frequently the result of stress, anxiety, a sudden change in lifestyle or the constant covering of the head.	Use a mild herbal shampoo every other day followed by a herbal or vinegar rinse. Use a herbal anti-dandruff lotion or conditioner daily or after each shampoo. Treat gently. Follow a high protein fruit and vegetable diet.	Burdock root, rosemary, southernwood, sage, goosegrass, stinging nettles, raspberry leaves, apple juice and herb vinegar.
ECZEMA AND ITCHY SCALP	True eczema is an unpleasant condition which requires professional treatment. An itchy scalp can be caused by inadequate rinsing after shampooing, frequent covering of the head, chemicals, chlorine, salt, central heating or an allergic reaction. Once you pinpoint the cause you can act to prevent recurrence.	Use a mild vinegar soak before shampooing. Use a herbal shampoo every other day followed by a herbal vinegar or lemon rinse. Use a scalp and hair conditioner regularly.	Essential oils of lavender, bergamot and juniper. Catmint, comfrey, nettle, parsley, raspberry leaves, quince, rosemary, southernwood, thyme and yarrow infusions. Witch hazel and flower water.

PROBLEMS AFFECTING YOUR HAIR

Anxiety, nervous tension and ill health can all affect the condition and quality of your hair. Many people suffer with excessively brittle hair, while others find that it is their scalp that is the problem. This chart shows several commonly occurring problems and acts as a guide to relevant treatments using naturally therapeutic hair products, which, if used regularly will restore your hair to its full health.

CAMOMILE AND SOAPWORT SHAMPOO

A gentle cleanser for problem hair.

15ml (1 tbsp) powdered soapwort root
15ml (1 tbsp) dried camomile flowers
275ml (½ pt) water

Boil the water and pour it over the herbs in a heatproof bowl. Leave the mixture to infuse overnight. Strain before use.

An infusion of soapwort – its root, leaves and stem – makes a soapy liquid which, although it does not lather, gently and thoroughly cleanses the hair. Any herb can be substituted for the camomile, depending on the problem being treated. An infusion of white dead nettles, for instance, makes a good shampoo treatment for oily hair.

A CONDITIONING SHAMPOO

An excellent thickening shampoo for dry and damaged hair.

30ml (2 tbsps) strong herbal infusion (see p20)
30ml (2 tbsps) liquid soap base (see p64)
1 egg
15ml (1 tbsp) powdered gelatine

Warm the infusion and whisk all the ingredients into it together, ensuring that they are well dissolved. Leave on your hair for 5-10 minutes. Rinse well with plenty of lukewarm water.

ORANGE AND EGG SHAMPOO

A good shampoo for oily, itchy scalps.

275ml (½ pt) strong soapwort infusion (see p20)
1 egg
15ml (1 tbsp) orange juice

Warm the infusion and beat the egg yolk and orange juice into it. Massage the mixture well into your hair and leave for 10 minutes. Rinse thoroughly with lukewarm water.

OIL PRE-CONDITIONER

A healing treatment for dry and damaged hair.

150ml (¼ pt) olive oil, sunflower oil, or suitable herbal oil (see p21)

Heat the oil gently in a *bain-marie* until it is blood temperature. Massage well into the scalp until your hair is completely saturated. Comb through with a wide-toothed comb. Massage again, then cover your hair in a plastic shower cap and swathe your head in a hot towel. Leave overnight for the best results. Shampoo with a mild baby shampoo.

HERBAL OIL PRE-CONDITIONER

Different essential oils can be used in this conditioner to suit the requirements of your hair – rosemary for falling hair and dandruff, cedarwood for thinning and lifeless hair, lavender, juniper or bergamot for an irritated scalp, verbena for oily hair and nettle for dandruff.

15ml (1 tbsp) anhydrous lanolin
15ml (1 tbsp) almond oil
15ml (1 tbsp) glycerine
2 drops any essential oil
1 egg yolk

Melt the lanolin in a bowl in a *bain-marie* and gently beat in the oils. Remove from the heat and beat in the egg yolk. Use as you would the Oil Pre-Conditioner, but leave for only 30 minutes.

ALMOND OIL AND HONEY CONDITIONER

Strengthens dry and damaged hair with split ends.

30ml (2 tbsps) almond oil
5ml (1 tsp) clear honey
1 egg yolk

Combine the oil and honey together and beat in the egg. Use as you would the Oil Pre-Conditioner, but leave for only 30 minutes.

CHAPTER THREE

HANDS AND FEET

The time spent on the care of your hands, feet and nails is often minimal compared to the hours lavished on your face and hair. Yet the skin on your hands and feet is particularly delicate. Beautiful hands and feet are rare assets that are well worth striving for and with a little concentrated treatment, including regular exercise, moisturizing, massage and nail care, you should see a marked improvement.

Because they are so often neglected, your hands and your feet tend to suffer from a host of problems, ranging from chilblains to corns and splitting nails. The advice and treatments prescribed in this chapter, using natural products, will help to soothe those troubles away and prevent their recurrence.

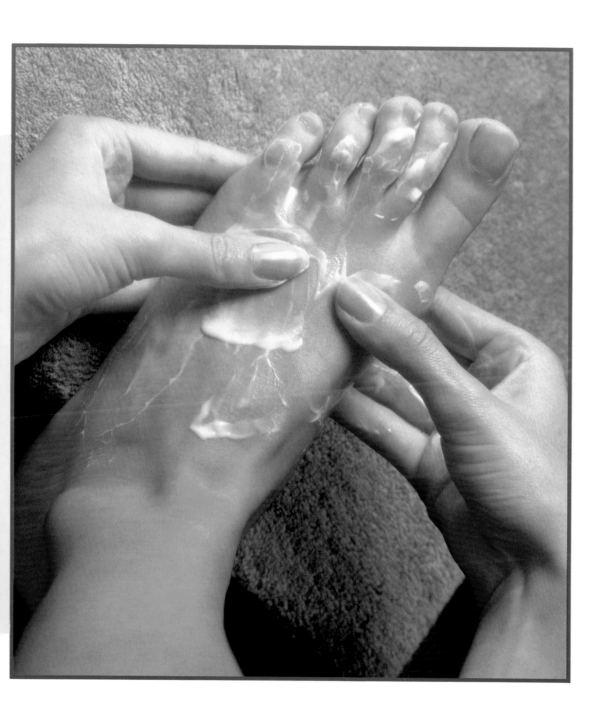

Hand care/1

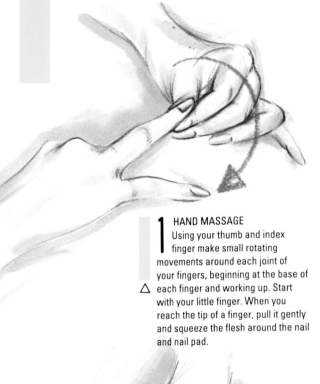

Your hands are often the focus of attention and their movements and appearance reveal a good deal about your character. Neglected hands and nails can ruin an otherwise elegant appearance, so keep them in tip-top condition.

There is little fatty tissue and few sebaceous glands to feed the skin on our hands, yet we constantly subject them to harsh detergents, dirt and water without a second thought and only occasionally dab on hand cream as a concession to skin care. You should treat the skin on your hands with as much respect as you do that on your face and body.

Ideally you should wear protective gloves for household chores and gardening. This is often inconvenient, however, so you should make sure that you wear a good barrier cream to minimize the chance of any damage. The greatest enemy of attractive hands and nails is dirt, so keep them scrupulously clean – rinsing and drying them thoroughly and always finishing off with plenty of hand cream.

As soon as you feel your hands becoming dry, reach for your hand cream. If their condition worsens, treat them to a rich night cream. Massage the cream in well and put on a pair of soft cotton gloves for warmth – and to protect your sheets. The skin on your hands will also benefit from a weekly mask. Use the same sort as you would for your face to get rid of deeply engrained dirt, smooth, bleach and soften your hands.

Massage and exercise are invaluable, not only to keep your fingers supple and stimulate the circulation but also to guard against stiffening of the joints, which can ultimately become crippling. Follow the outlines described on these pages regularly to keep your hands supple and smooth.

1 HAND MASSAGE
Using your thumb and index finger make small rotating movements around each joint of your fingers, beginning at the base of each finger and working up. Start with your little finger. When you reach the tip of a finger, pull it gently and squeeze the flesh around the nail and nail pad.

2 Stroke down the finger and down the back of your hand.

3 Massage from the thumb knuckle down to the wrist using the same rotary movement and continue it around the wrist.

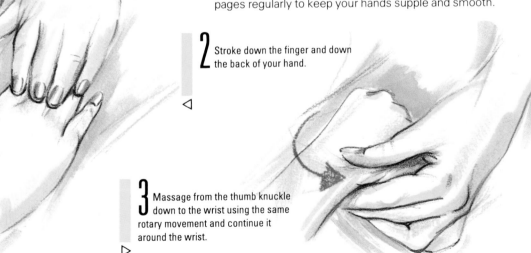

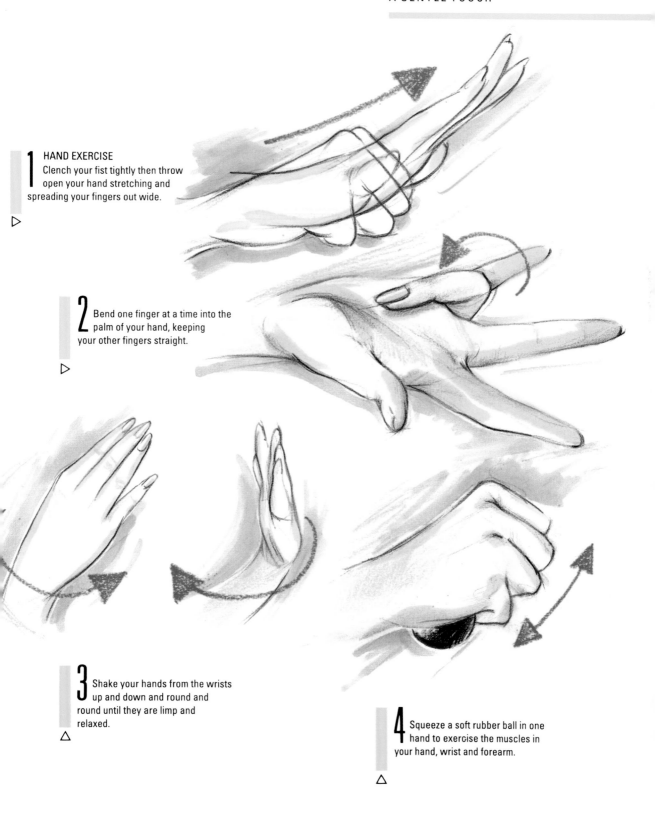

1 HAND EXERCISE
Clench your fist tightly then throw open your hand stretching and spreading your fingers out wide.

▷

2 Bend one finger at a time into the palm of your hand, keeping your other fingers straight.

▷

3 Shake your hands from the wrists up and down and round and round until they are limp and relaxed.

△

4 Squeeze a soft rubber ball in one hand to exercise the muscles in your hand, wrist and forearm.

△

SIMPLE SECRETS

To clean and whiten:

A little sugar in 15ml (1 tablespoon) of oil rubbed into the hands removes ingrained dirt and stains, leaving them very smooth.

To soften:

Keep the fat from the Christmas goose and rub it into your hands frequently to make them soft and white.
A pinch of bicarbonate of soda, borax or 15ml (1 tablespoon) of vinegar in a bowl of water will soften the skin of your hands.

To bleach:

Fruit pulp is full of pectin and acid and makes a wonderfully efficient hand whitening mask. Use the residue left after making fruit jelly.

ROSEWATER AND GLYCERINE BARRIER LOTION

A softening, mildly bleaching protective cream.

150ml (¼ pt) rosewater
75ml (5 tbsps) glycerine
30ml (2 tbsps) pure lemon juice – optional
5ml (1 tsp) clear honey – optional

Put all the ingredients in a bottle, shake well and use frequently. Lemon juice bleaches and softens hands, but, like glycerine, it may sting if your skin is chapped. Keep the squeezed lemon halves to rub on your elbows for a thorough cleanse.

ORANGE FLOWER HAND JELLY

A light, inexpensive all-purpose jelly. Rosewater or elderflower water *(see p20)* can be substituted for the orange flower water.

15ml (1 tbsp) glycerine
10ml (2 tsps) arrowroot
75ml (5 tbsps) orange flower water

Place the glycerine in a bowl and the orange flower water in another. Heat them both to the same temperature in a *bain-marie*. Add the arrowroot very carefully to the glycerine to make a thick, smooth cream. Gradually add the warm orange flower water to the glycerine mixture stirring continuously over the heat until the mixture clears to form a thick jelly.

LANOLIN HAND CREAM

A rich thick protective cream.

45ml (3 tbsps) anhydrous lanolin
30ml (2 tbsps) almond oil
30ml (2 tbsps) glycerine
few drops of geranium or sandalwood oil

Warm the lanolin in a bowl in a *bain-marie*. Beat in the almond oil and glycerine. Continue beating the mixture until it cools and add the drops of perfumed oil.

HONEY HAND CREAM

A rich and nourishing cream.

150g (6oz) anhydrous lanolin
75g (3oz) clear honey
90ml (6 tbsps) almond oil

Melt the lanolin in a *bain-marie* and whisk in the honey. Remove from the heat and beat in the almond oil. Beat the mixture continuously until it cools. Pot and seal.

LANOLIN AND SESAME NIGHT CREAM

A creamy overnight conditioner which should be massaged into your hands. Wear cotton gloves for increased absorption.

45ml (3 tbsps) anhydrous lanolin
15ml (1 tbsp) sesame oil

Melt the lanolin in a bowl in a *bain-marie*. Beat in the sesame oil and remove from the heat. Beat the mixture continuously until cool and creamy. Pot and seal.

ALMOND AND HONEY NIGHT OIL

A rich, oily overnight conditioner which should be massaged into your hands. Wear cotton gloves for increased absorption.

15ml (1 tbsp) almond oil
15ml (1 tbsp) olive oil
5ml (1 tsp) clear honey
7.5ml (½ tbsp) glycerine

Warm the oils with the honey in a bowl in a *bain-marie* until they are well mixed together. Remove from the heat and beat in the glycerine. Bottle and seal.

PLAIN ALL-PURPOSE HAND AND FACE CREAM

An old-fashioned but very effective cream.

30ml (2 tbsps) vegetable lard
30ml (2 tbsps) olive oil
60ml (4 tbsps) sunflower oil
few drops of perfumed oil

Melt the lard in a bowl in a *bain-marie* and beat in the oils. Beat the mixture continuously until it is cool and add the perfumed oil. Pot and seal.

OLIVE OIL HAND BATH

Olive oil soothes and smoothes hands wonderfully well and helps to "rejuvenate" older hands which are becoming wrinkled. This bath is also a balm for hands roughened and dry as a result of hard work.

275ml (½ pt) olive oil

Warm the olive oil in a bowl in a *bain-marie*. Remove from the heat and sit with your hands in it for as long as possible. Massage them well before removing the excess oil with a tissue. Give your elbows a treat with the same bath.

OLIVE OIL AND OATMEAL PASTE

A wonderful way to make your hands smooth for a special occasion.

15ml (1 tbsp) fine ground oatmeal
5ml (1 tsp) warm water
5ml (1 tsp) olive oil
5ml (1 tsp) lemon juice
5ml (1 tsp) glycerine

Mix all the ingredients together. Smooth this paste over your hands and leave for 10 minutes. Rinse off well.

NAIL CARE/1

Nails are made from *keratin* – the same dead cell substance which coats hair shafts – so they cannot be nourished externally. We can improve their condition by sticking to a healthy diet and treating the cuticle area with care.

The growing nail cells form just beneath the cuticle in the *matrix*, a tiny part of which can be seen in the pale half moon or *lunula* at the base of the nail, and this area is particularly sensitive to damage. Jarring the nail at its tip can injure the cuticle, as can careless clipping and banging or probing of the matrix, resulting in permanent damage to the growing nail. This manifests itself in the appearance of white flecks, ridges and in weak, splitting nails. In the worst cases the nail may be lost, as those of us who have slammed our fingers in a door will know.

Illness and poor health can also show in the poor condition of our nails. The same healthy diet – rich in protein, fresh fruits and vegetables and supplemented with Vitamin B – which is essential for healthy skin, hair and general well-being, also ensures healthy nails. One tablespoon of unflavoured gelatine a day improves the strength of nails.

Your nails must be well kept if your hands are to look beautiful. Careful treatment is essential to achieve the ideal – a perfectly pale almond-shaped nail, with straight sides and smoothly tapered tip. Every time you wash your hands, gently push the cuticle back with your towel as you dry them. When applying hand cream, massage a little into the base of the nail to keep the cuticle soft and stimulate the blood flow to feed the growing nail. File your nails into shape with an emery board, using the fine side. Do not use cuticle clippers, metal probes or nail files to keep your nails in shape because they can cause damage.

Cuticles should be eased from the nail surface not brutalized by cutting or rough pulling, which only result in torn skin and painful hangnails. Try to avoid bringing harsh nail varnish removers into contact with your cuticles, as this might affect the condition of your nails. Keep your cuticles soft and strengthen your nails by massaging in a cuticle cream regularly, or painting with a conditioning lotion every night. A weekly manicure will help to ensure problem-free hands and nails.

Smooth, pale pink, almond-shaped fingernails can be yours if you keep your nails in peak condition, using natural strengtheners and cuticle conditioners. A chamois polisher stimulates nail growth as it buffs your nails to a healthy, attractive shine.

OILY CUTICLE SOFTENER

15ml (1 tbsp) castor oil
15ml (1 tbsp) glycerine

Mix the ingredients together and massage into the cuticle before soaking for a manicure.

CUTICLE SOFTENER

A softening mixture for hard cuticle skin. Do not use on sore or chapped hands.

30ml (2 tbsps) pineapple juice
2 beaten egg yolks
5ml (1 tsp) cider vinegar

Mix the ingredients together and soak your nails in the mixture for 30 minutes.

LANOLIN PASTE

A paste that polishes nails to a pinky glow.

30ml (2 tbsps) anhydrous lanolin
5ml (1 tsp) kaolin
5ml (1 tsp) lecithin powder
2 drops oil of geranium

Mix the ingredients together and massage into your
nails. Wipe the surplus off with a soft cloth and buff your
nails to a shine.

NOURISHING NIGHT CREAM

5ml (1 tsp) clear honey
5ml (1 tsp) avocado or almond oil
5ml (1 tsp) beaten egg yolk

Mix the ingredients together and massage into your
nails. Put on a pair of cotton gloves and allow the cream
to penetrate overnight.

LEMON AND IODINE LOTION

This lotion strengthens nails and discourages nail biting.
Lemon or iodine can be used separately with equally
good results.

10ml (2 tsps) iodine
10ml (2 tsps) lemon juice

Mix the ingredients together and paint the lotion on to
your nails.

NAIL CARE/2

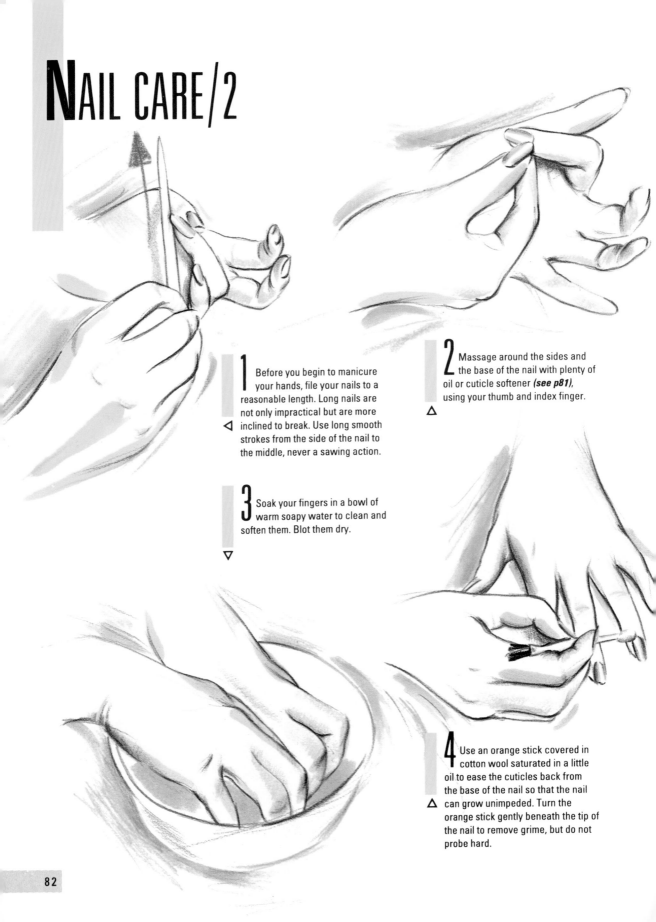

1 Before you begin to manicure your hands, file your nails to a reasonable length. Long nails are not only impractical but are more ◁ inclined to break. Use long smooth strokes from the side of the nail to the middle, never a sawing action.

2 Massage around the sides and the base of the nail with plenty of oil or cuticle softener *(see p81)*, using your thumb and index finger.
△

3 Soak your fingers in a bowl of warm soapy water to clean and soften them. Blot them dry.
▽

4 Use an orange stick covered in cotton wool saturated in a little oil to ease the cuticles back from the base of the nail so that the nail △ can grow unimpeded. Turn the orange stick gently beneath the tip of the nail to remove grime, but do not probe hard.

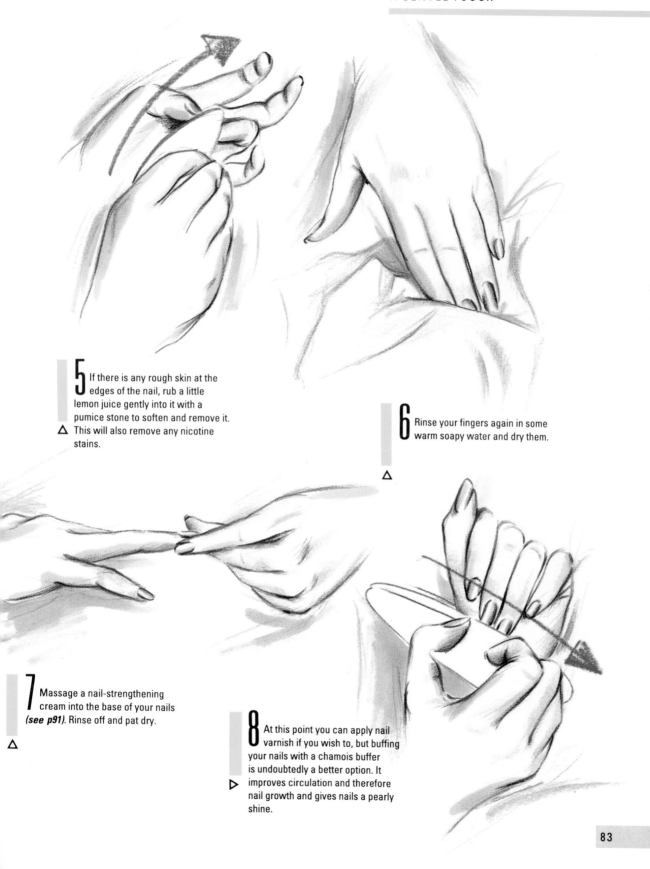

5 If there is any rough skin at the edges of the nail, rub a little lemon juice gently into it with a pumice stone to soften and remove it.
△ This will also remove any nicotine stains.

6 Rinse your fingers again in some warm soapy water and dry them.
△

7 Massage a nail-strengthening cream into the base of your nails *(see p91)*. Rinse off and pat dry.
△

8 At this point you can apply nail varnish if you wish to, but buffing your nails with a chamois buffer is undoubtedly a better option. It improves circulation and therefore nail growth and gives nails a pearly shine.
▷

FOOT CARE/1

The complaint, 'My feet are killing me' is not in fact as far-fetched as it sounds because your feet can be the source of pain and tension throughout your body. Ill-fitting shoes and lack of localized exercise can damage the muscular structure of your feet and throw your frame off-balance. High heels and badly made footwear distort the natural weight of your body and bring pressure to bear on the wrong parts of your feet and legs, which leads to aching veins and joints, backache and nervous strain. It is, therefore, vitally important that you pay particular attention to foot care if you are to avoid exacerbation of these problems.

One of the most pleasurable pain-relieving and relaxing treatments is a foot massage *(see p87)*. There are small points all over our feet which relate to different parts of the body. Imagine your foot is a map of your body and press gently in the area that corresponds to the stressed area of your body for instant relief.

Exercising your feet daily *(see p86)* reduces the possibility of foot-related strains. When you get home change into flat shoes or walk barefoot. Learning to treat yourself through regular exercise and massage will minimize the ill-effects of everyday wear and tear.

Looking after your feet also requires careful attention to hygiene and nail care. Wash your feet every.day in warm water and massage with a cream or oil. This relaxes tense muscles and stimulates the blood flow, thus reducing the risk of chilblains and other circulatory problems. Keep your toenails short. Cut them straight across when they are softened after a wash. Do not attempt to shape them as this can result in ingrowing toenails. Smooth off the edges of your nails with the coarse side of an emery board. Give yourself a pedicure every week following the same guidelines as described for the manicure *(see pp82-3)*.

When your feet hurt and your ankles are swollen soak them in a warm remedial foot bath and then lie down with them slightly raised on a cushion. This is a miracle cure.

If you develop a persistent problem, such as corns, broken chilblains or verrucas, then visit a chiropodist immediately to prevent the condition deteriorating to a serious degree.

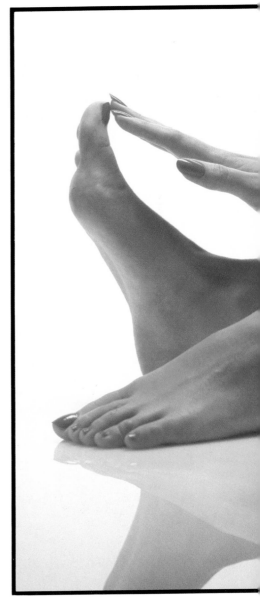

SIMPLE SECRETS
For aching feet:
100g (4oz) sea salt or 15ml (1 tablespoon) washing soda to a basin of warm water to soothe aching feet.

To soothe away the cold:
5ml (1 teaspoon) mustard powder to a basin hot water when cold, wet and tired.

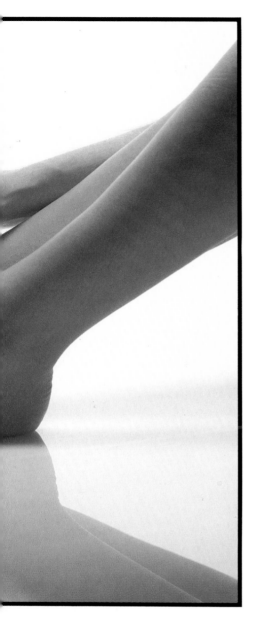

Fill a basin with warm water and add the salts and the borax. Soak your feet until the water is cold. Dry your feet, then massage them thoroughly with witch hazel, concentrating on the sides of the feet.

HERBAL FOOT BATH

A relaxing treat for tired feet. Crushed juniper, rosemary and lavender make an especially good mixture.

15ml (1 tbsp) washing soda or 63g (2½ oz) sea salt
1 handful of any mixture of mint, yarrow, marigold
   leaves, peppermint, camomile, lavender, rosemary,
   thyme and lime flowers

Infuse the herbs in boiling water and add this infusion to a basin of warm water with the soda or salt.

YOGHURT FOOT PACK

A softening, whitening treatment for hardened, discoloured skin.

150ml (¼ pt) natural yoghurt
5ml (1 tsp) malt vinegar

Mix the ingredients together and brush all over the feet, ankles and heels. Leave for five minutes and rinse off.

CLOVE MASSAGE OIL

A tension-relieving treat.

45ml (3 tbsps) olive oil or sunflower oil
4 drops oil of cloves

Mix the oils together and massage well into the feet.

LAVENDER MASSAGE OIL

Also relieves tension. Lavender oil and flowers added to a foot bath are very therapeutic.

45ml (3 tbsps) almond oil
3 drops oil of lavender

Mix the oils together and massage into the feet.

FOOT CREAM

A soothing, emollient balm.

90ml (6 tbsps) anhydrous lanolin
45ml (3 tbsps) almond oil
45ml (3 tbsps) glycerine
2 drops oil of geranium or lavender – optional

Melt the lanolin in a bowl in a *bain-marie* then beat in the oil and the glycerine. Beat the mixture until it is nearly cool and add the perfume if you wish. Pot and seal.

FOOT BATH

A good method of soothing and hardening the feet. It is especially useful for keen walkers and athletes, or when you wear plimsoles, rubber flip flops and summer sandals, or if you choose to go barefoot.

30ml (2 tbsps) Epsom salts
15ml (1 tbsp) borax
witch hazel

FOOT CARE/2

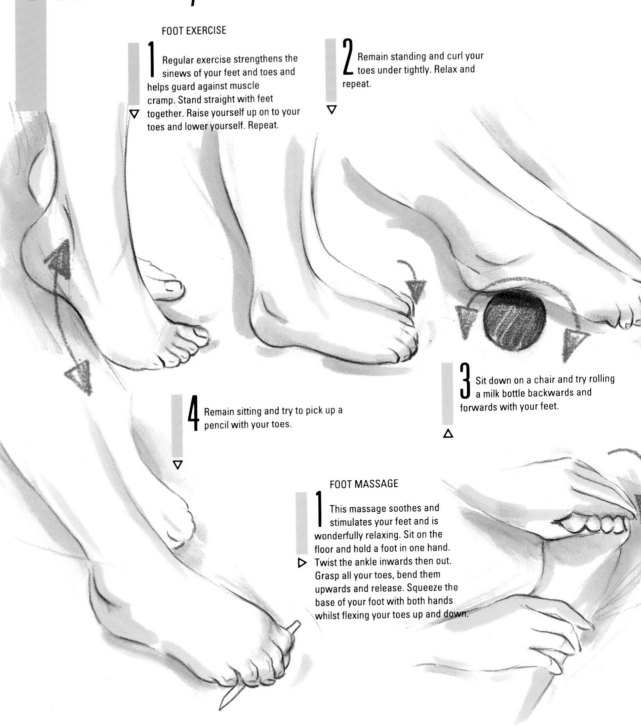

FOOT EXERCISE

1 Regular exercise strengthens the sinews of your feet and toes and helps guard against muscle cramp. Stand straight with feet together. Raise yourself up on to your toes and lower yourself. Repeat.

2 Remain standing and curl your toes under tightly. Relax and repeat.

3 Sit down on a chair and try rolling a milk bottle backwards and forwards with your feet.

4 Remain sitting and try to pick up a pencil with your toes.

FOOT MASSAGE

1 This massage soothes and stimulates your feet and is wonderfully relaxing. Sit on the floor and hold a foot in one hand. Twist the ankle inwards then out. Grasp all your toes, bend them upwards and release. Squeeze the base of your foot with both hands whilst flexing your toes up and down.

2 With cream or oil on your hands, pull each toe gently away from its neighbour and follow the pulling and rotating routine suggested for the fingers in the hand massage *(see p76)*. Continue stroking up from the toes to the ankle.

3 Press your thumb along the top of the foot, pushing gently at the base of each toe.

4 Stroke, pinch and knead the sides and sole of the foot, concentrating on the stress-related areas.

5 Using the thumb of one hand and the fingers of the other, make small pressing, rotating movements on each side of the ankle. Continue up around the Achilles tendon, the sides of the heel and down the side of the upper sole and arch of your foot, then back again to the ankle. Do the same on the other foot, then wiggle both feet in the air.

PROBLEMS SOLVED/4

PROBLEMS AFFECTING HANDS, FEET AND NAILS.
The distressing, painful problems that affect hands and feet are largely the result of poor circulation, an inadequate diet or neglect. Natural remedies have been tried and tested throughout the years and are often the simplest way to soothe any discomfort. This chart outlines the basic treatments for a range of problems.

	CHAPPED HANDS	*CHILBLAINS*	*CORNS AND CALLOUSES*
CAUSE	The rough red, sometimes split skin on fingers and knuckles typical of this problem is caused by subjecting your hands to very hot and cold water, leaving them damp, using harsh detergents and exposing them to cold wind.	Chilblains are swollen red patches surrounded by pale skin and are itchy and painful. They are caused by inadequate protection from extremes of temperature, poor circulation and sometimes poor diet. They are more common on feet than on hands, and usually appear on heels and joints. In severe cases the chilblains can break causing extreme discomfort.	Corns are small areas of thickened skin which develop on toes. Callouses are larger and usually develop on the soles of the feet. Both are caused by tight or ill-fitting shoes. Corns on the joints of the hands and callouses on the palms are usually caused by manual work.
SIMPLE TREATMENT	Rinse your hands thoroughly in borax solution. Dry them well and wear gloves. Use a barrier cream constantly. Massage with a rich cream or oil nightly.	Avoid extremes of temperature. Soak the affected areas daily in a warm remedial bath. Dry well and massage with a suitable herbal ointment. If the skin is broken, avoid using anything but a plain oil, such as olive or almond. Incorporate fresh fruit and vegetables in your diet. Apply herbal compresses to ease any pain.	Make sure that your shoes fit properly. Hard skin can be pared gently away or softened with a poultice. Visit a chiropodist if the problem persists.
HEALING INGREDIENTS	Cucumber, glycerine, honey, wheatgerm, lanolin and cocoa butter.	Marigold, onion, houseleek, alum, potato, elderflower and strawberry.	Garlic, tomato, iodine and marigold.

SIMPLE SECRETS

Sensitive dry skin:
Use oatmeal, mixed to a smooth paste with a little water, as an alternative to soap. This also whitens the skin.

Sore feet:
Bring relief to aching feet by dabbing them with cucumber juice, or soak them in a basin of strong nettle infusion *(see p20)* containing 15ml (1 tablespoon) of cider vinegar.
Soothe blisters with a thick layer of cornflour paste. Dust alum powder on tired feet to refresh and harden them.

Excessive perspiration:
Half a teaspoon of alum in 275ml (½ pint) of warm water is an efficient deodorizer, as is a strong infusion of cleavers.
A few drops of essential oil of lemon grass added to a bowl of warm water as a soak, or 3 drops of lemon grass oil to 5ml (1 teaspoon) of sunflower oil as a massage oil guard against excessively perspiring feet.

Corns and callouses:
Crushed marigold leaves or marigold sap applied morning and night removes corns, callouses and soft warts.
Paint corns and callouses with tincture of iodine to soften and reduce them. Soothe painful corns with a piece of cotton wool soaked in turpentine.
A slice of raw tomato will soften corns if bandaged against them.
Rubbing corns with raw garlic will reduce them.
Soft corns between toes should be well washed, dried and dusted with unscented baby talc.

Chilblains:
An elderflower compress will relieve pain.
Strawberry juice is a good preventative, as is a poultice of the crushed fruit.
Roast figs ground with honey makes a soothing and luxurious paste for hands with chilblains.
A nightly poultice of a small onion chopped and boiled in a little water, or a poultice of grated raw potato, will bring relief.

Chapped skin:
Apply a solution of equal parts cucumber juice and witch hazel.
Soak your hands in a bowl of warm milk.
Glycerine rubbed into your hands will make them sting, but is ultimately a very effective treatment. Massage wheatgerm oil into the hands and cover them with cotton gloves overnight to heal sore, splitting hands.

DRY FLAKING SKIN

This condition on the hands is usually caused by detergents and insufficient rinsing and drying, although it often accompanies a generally dry skin type. It can also be caused by central heating. When it occurs on your feet or legs, it is usually caused by the friction of tights or boots.

Add vinegar to a basin of water to rinse your hands. Massage well with honey and/or oil daily. Avoid using soap and remove any dirt with a mixture of sugar and olive oil.

Honey, lanolin (test for allergy) and oil. Comfrey, marigold, nettles and quince seeds.

SPLIT NAILS

Split nails are caused by insufficient care of the cuticle or bad filing. Nails can become brittle as a result of poor nourishment and exposure to abrasive detergents.

Use a nail-strengthening lotion daily and a nourishing cuticle cream nightly. Keep your cuticles soft. Supplement your diet with Vitamin B and unflavoured gelatine.

Olive oil, lecithin, lanolin, iodine, lemon juice.

OLIVE OIL MASSAGE CREAM

A cream to help alleviate dry and flaking skin on your feet and legs.

30ml (2 tbsps) anhydrous lanolin
30ml (2 tbsps) olive oil

Melt the lanolin in a bowl in a *bain-marie*. Beat in the olive oil and then leave the mixture to cool. Pot and seal. Use nightly.

HONEY TREATMENT FOR DRY SKIN

This is an especially effective remedy for dry skin on your knees and elbows.

75ml (5 tbsps) clear honey

Warm the honey and rub it into the affected area, having washed with warm water. Leave the honey on your skin for 30 minutes. Rinse it off and pat your skin dry.

HONEY PASTE FOR DRY SKIN

A good treatment for dry, dirt ingrained skin on hands, feet, elbows and knees.

15ml (1 tbsp) clear honey
1 egg white
5ml (1 tsp) glycerine
fine ground oatmeal

Mix the first three ingredients together with enough oatmeal to make a paste. Apply where necessary and leave for 30 minutes before bathing.

POTATO HAND AND FOOT MASK

A whitening. softening treatment which also reduces chilblains and swollen joints.

2 large potatoes
15ml (1 tbsp) milk
5ml (1 tsp) glycerine
5ml (1 tsp) rose water

Boil and mash the potatoes. Add the other ingredients while the potato is still warm. Apply the mixture to the hands and feet and leave for an hour. Use this treatment regularly for best results.

MARIGOLD BATH

A soothing treatment for chilblains.

2l (3½pts) marigold decoction (see p20)
2 handfuls sea salt

Warm the mixture and bathe your hands in it whilst still tepid as a precaution against chilblains. This can be used again and again as a daily treatment.

TREATMENT FOR CORNS AND CALLOUSES

This also makes an effective balm for tender feet.

30ml (2 tbsps) bicarbonate of soda
45ml (3 tbsps) sunflower oil
10ml (2 tsps) cider vinegar

Dissolve the bicarbonate in a basin of warm water. Soak your feet in it until the water cools. Mix the oil and the vinegar and use the mixture to massage into the affected areas.

ORRIS ROOT AND OATMEAL POWDER

A dusting powder for moist and perspiring hands and feet.

120ml (8 tbsps) fine ground oatmeal
30ml (2 tbsps) orris root powder

Mix the ingredients together and pass them through a fine sieve. Keep in a sealed pot and use to dust your hands and feet.

HONEY LOTION

A soothing treatment for very rough dry hands.

30ml (2 tbsps) clear honey
30ml (2 tbsps) almond or sesame oil
75ml (5 tbsps) rosewater
15ml (1 tbsp) cider vinegar

Warm the honey in a bowl in a *bain-marie* and beat in the oil. Remove the mixture from the heat. Add the rosewater slowly, followed by the vinegar and beat the mixture constantly until it cools. Bottle and seal.

MARIGOLD JELLY

A very effective remedy for sore or sunburnt hands and for chilblains on hands and feet. It also soothes hangnails and cracked skin.

6 fresh marigold heads
1 large jar petroleum jelly

Clean and break up the flower heads. Melt the petroleum jelly in a bowl in a *bain-marie*. Add the marigolds and simmer gently for several hours. Strain the mixture and pot.

COCOA BUTTER CONDITIONING CREAM

An oily soothing cream for rough and reddened hands which can also be used on elbows, knees and feet.

30ml (2 tbsps) cocoa butter
30ml (2 tbsps) anhydrous lanolin
75ml (5 tbsps) sunflower oil

Melt the ingredients together in a *bain-marie*. Pot and seal once cool.

CARE FOR PROBLEM NAILS
SIMPLE SECRETS
To strengthen:
Steep your nails in a strong infusion *(see p20)*, of dill or elm leaves, or cider vinegar, to strengthen them.

OLIVE OIL AND LECITHIN CREAM

A cream which strengthens brittle nails.

10ml (2 tsps) olive oil
10ml (2 tsps) lecithin powder

Mix the ingredients to a smooth paste. Massage into your nails and leave for 30 minutes or overnight.

LANOLIN NAIL STRENGTHENER

For dry and splitting nails.

15ml (1 tbsp) anhydrous lanolin
2.5ml (½ tsp) iodine

Melt the lanolin in a *bain-marie* and stir in the iodine. Pot and seal once cool. Rub into your cuticles and leave on for as long as possible.

CHAPTER FOUR

THE BODY

We are not all lucky enough to have a perfect body, but with careful grooming, regular exercise and a healthy diet we can certainly make the most of the one we have been given. Your body will respond as soon as you start a concentrated care programme and your self-confidence will increase.

Protecting yourself from the sun should be a priority if you value the condition of your skin. It is only too tempting to try and establish a glamorous suntan, but great care must be taken if permanent damage is to be avoided. Keep an eye on your children's skin when they are out in the sun too – their skin needs even more protection. Keeping the skin on your face and body in good condition all-year-round is essential if it is to withstand the different climatic and environmental changes it will experience from season to season, so treat yourself to naturally rich conditioning creams.

Body Basics

If you are to make the most of your body's potential for healthy beauty, you must be prepared to spend time and effort bringing it to peak condition. Your diet is of paramount importance because without a sufficient intake of the essential vitamins, minerals and proteins you cannot hope to develop a vibrantly healthy physique. Regular exercise, preferably in the open air, is the perfect way to keep yourself in shape and promote a sense of well-being. The third step on the road to self-improvement is to cultivate a thorough cleansing, moisturizing and massage routine, so that the inner health of your body shines out.

DIET

This book would not be complete if it did not include some guidelines regarding the correct diet for maximum beauty potential. All the raw natural ingredients which work such wonders on our skin, hair, teeth, eyes and nails are equally beneficial to our body. Without their regular intake to form the basis for healthy and natural good looks, all cosmetic efforts will be in vain.

A healthy habit

Once you have learnt which foods do you the most good, you should begin to include them in your daily diet and gradually establish an entirely healthy eating routine. If you do not have the time to cook regular meals, a substantial breakfast is a must.

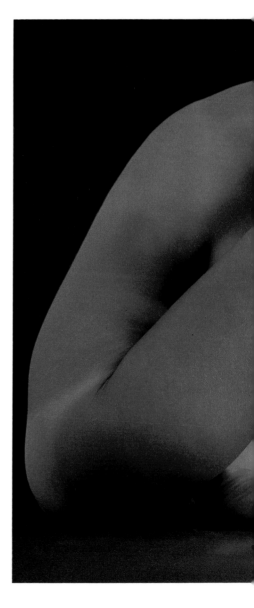

This recipe provides a first-class, highly nutritious breakfast food:

450g (1lb) raw porridge oats
450g (1lb) raisins
225g (½lb) wheat flakes
100g (4oz) wheatgerm
100g (4oz) mixed chopped nuts (not peanuts)
100g (4oz) dried banana chips (crushed)
100g (4oz) sesame seeds
50g (2oz) pumpkin seeds
50g (2oz) sunflower seeds

Mix all the ingredients together and serve with chopped fresh fruit, stewed dried fruit, fruit juice, yoghurt or milk. This should make enough to last you a month.

Eating at least one salad a day is an easy way to ensure a good intake of important vitamins. Vary the style of salad you make by incorporating a host of different raw vegetables – celery, tomatoes, carrots, courgettes, fennel, cauliflower, parsley, cucumber, red and green peppers and lettuce – and

Your inner health shines out through the gleam of your body's skin and its muscle tone. Keep your body looking its best with natural cleansers and tonics, a healthy diet and regular exercise.

dress it with an olive oil, garlic and herb vinegar dressing. The addition of an assortment of oranges, beansprouts, walnuts, sweetcorn or peaches makes for an unusual and wholesome salad treat. You may enjoy your salad on its own, or prefer to eat it with a hard boiled egg, cheese, fish or chicken and wholemeal bread or crispbread.

Plain yoghurt and fresh or dried fruits should always be on your daily menu. Try to reduce your intake of alcohol, coffee and tea and replace these drinks with fruit juices, purified water and herbal teas. An evening cup of soothing lemon tea with a large spoonful of honey stirred into it is a wonderful way to ease the tensions of the day.

Establish a regular exercise routine that suits your needs and your lifestyle. Walking, swimming and yoga are all excellent and enjoyable ways of keeping fit.

Dieting

There are innumerable books and theories on this subject and the pressure to go on a diet can be immense. If for any reason dieting makes you unhappy, do not do it, unless you have to for health reasons and then only under medical supervision. There are many plump, beautiful women in the world whose calm radiance comes from accepting the fact that health and happiness are not exclusive to slender women. It is likely that you will be neither healthy nor happy if you force yourself to be perpetually hungry and deprive your body of the necessary vitamins, minerals, proteins and oils. Cutting out meals is no guarantee that you will slim successfully and results in the temptation to overeat when your will-power cracks. Ensure instead that the food you *do* eat is the correct food in terms of energy value and nutritional content.

If you covet a svelte silhouette then the easiest way to achieve it is to cut down the size of your meals, gradually substituting large portions of raw vegetables and fruit for those foods which you know to be fattening. These raw foods need to be thoroughly chewed and therefore reduce the fatal desire to nibble between meals. If you do still feel the urge to have the occasional snack, try unsalted nuts, seeds and dried fruit instead of artificially flavoured biscuits, crisps and sweets. These are all delicious and very nourishing. Indulging yourself in this way will gradually reduce your craving for quick unhealthy snacks.

EXERCISE

Taking plenty of exercise reinforces the good effects of a sensible diet. Again there are many books available on this subject and it is best to be guided by one that caters for your age group. Energetic dance exercises are fine if you are in your teens or twenties and are used to disco-dancing, but there is no benefit to be had from a daily plunge through the pain barrier if your body is completely unused to such exertion. Take things gently at first and work up to the stage where you feel that you can tackle something more strenuous.

Walking, swimming and cycling are the best exercises to keep you in good all-over physical shape. The degree of exertion involved in these methods of exercise is for you to choose, according to your personal level of fitness. Build up your strength and stamina day by day and establish a routine that suits you.

Whichever type of exercise you choose to take, whether it be running, isometrics, yoga or jazz dancing, be careful not to overextend yourself before you are ready. You could do yourself more harm than good.

BODY POLISH

A shower or a quick bath every day is a necessity for reasons of hygiene, but a longer soak in a warm, aromatic bath from time to time can bring you tremendous therapeutic and cosmetic benefits.

Tension, bad temper, anxiety, aches and pains are soothed away in the bath. Your skin is polished and stimulated by gentle scrubbing with a good soap, or smoothed and healed by the addition of lotions and infusions to your bath water. Warm heady fumes resulting from the addition of aromatic oils to a steaming bath can induce a feeling of peace and well-being, further encouraged by a relaxing massage with fragrant and conditioning body oils.

LUXURY CLEANSING

SOAP

There are several ways of making your own soap, but these recipes follow the simplest and least hazardous method. Vary the type of soap you make with the different types of herbal infusions, flower waters *(see p20)*, perfumes and colours you use. The addition of honey to the basic soap makes it a soothing cleanser, while oatmeal will add an abrasive quality. Infusions of herbs can be added to treat specific skin conditions *(see pp18-19)*, complemented with appropriate perfumed oils. Luxurious scented soaps can be made with the addition of flower waters and their corresponding perfumed oil. Colours can be added with the perfume to give the soaps a special appeal.

Use small, wax-lined plastic containers as moulds. While the soap is hardening in its mould, cover it with a damp towel to prevent cracking and keep it in a warm, dry place for two to four weeks. Different types of soap take longer to set than others, so do not worry if your soap seems slow to harden.

Bath oils

You can make a wonderfully relaxing bath oil with any vegetable oil, plus either a herbal oil *(see p21)*, or a fragrant essential oil, such as rose, lemon grass or geranium.

Herbal baths

Take a selection of herbs and place them in a small, simple linen drawstring bag. Hang the bag on the tap so that it is suspended beneath the running hot water and the herbal essences will flow into the bath.

Add orange and lemon peel or cloves to the herbal mixture to give a spicy flavour to your bath. Bran, oatmeal or pearl barley can be added to the mixture to soften rough skin.

Bath-time herbs

Use these herbs to make oils or in bags for the bath of your choice:

Lemon balm, verbena and mint to soothe and cool.
Peppermint, pine, rosemary, thyme and eucalyptus leaves to invigorate.
Elderflowers, blackberry and geranium leaves to rejuvenate.
Yarrow, comfrey and marigold to soothe and heal
Camomile, elder and lime flowers plus powdered milk to soften and relax.

SIMPLE SECRETS

To soothe:
5ml (1 teaspoon) clear honey added to the bath rejuvenates and soothes.

To condition:
150ml (¼ pint) cider vinegar added to the bath restores the acid mantle of your skin, reduces irritation and increases the suppleness of your skin – especially helpful for expectant mothers.

To ease irritations:
10ml (2 teaspoons) bicarbonate of soda added to the bath reduces irritation.

To smooth:
15ml (1 tablespoon) laundry starch plus 5ml (1 teaspoon) glycerine added to the bath leaves your skin smooth and silky.

To relax:
Epsoms salts added to the bath soothe and relax.

BASIC HERBAL SOAP

Select the herbal infusion or flower water according to the condition of your skin.

450g (1lb) soap flakes or grated Castile or olive oil soap.
275ml (½pt) herbal infusion or flower water *(see p20)*
few drops perfumed oil

Melt the soap flakes and the infusion together in a pan over a gentle heat, stirring continuously until they are completely fluid. Remove from the heat and leave it to cool a little. Add the perfume and pour into the moulds. Leave to harden.

HONEY AND HERB SOAP

A soothing, mild cleanser.

250g (9oz) soap flakes or grated Castile or olive oil soap
275ml (½pt) herbal infusion or flower water (see p20)
120ml (8 tbsps) clear honey
few drops perfumed oil

Melt the soap flakes and the infusion together in a pan over a gentle heat, stirring continuously. Warm the honey in a bowl in a *bain-marie* and add it to the soap mixture, stirring well. When the mixture cools, add the perfume. Pour into the moulds and leave to harden.

OATMEAL AND HERB SOAP

A slightly abrasive cleanser.

250g (9oz) soap flakes or grated Castile or olive oil soap
275ml (½pt) herbal infusion or flower water (see p20)
100g (2oz) finely ground oatmeal
few drops perfumed oil

Melt the soap flakes and infusion together in a pan over a gentle heat, stirring continuously. Add the oatmeal immediately, making sure it is well mixed in. Remove from the heat and add a few drops of perfume when the mixture cools. Pour it into the moulds and leave to harden.

ROSEMARY BATH OIL

Any home-made herbal oil *(see p21)* or essential oil can be substituted for the rosemary.

60ml (4 tbsps) Turkey Red oil
15ml (1 tbsp) rosemary oil, or several drops of essential oil of rosemary.

Shake both ingredients together in a bottle. Add 15ml (1 tbsp) to your bath.

ALMOND BATH OIL

A luxurious foaming bath oil.

150ml (¼pt) almond oil
15ml (1 tbsp) clear baby shampoo
few drops essential oil for perfume

Shake the ingredients together in a bottle and shake before using. Add 15ml (1 tbsp) to your bath.

HONEY BATH

This oil disperses rapidly through the bath water.

75ml (5 tbsps) almond oil
5ml (1 tsp) clear honey
few drops essential oil for perfume
15ml (1 tbsp) alcohol

Shake the ingredients together in a bottle and pour 5ml (1 tsp) into the bath beneath running hot water.

BUBBLE BATH

A luxurious, skin-smoothing treat.

1 egg
75ml (5 tbsps) clear baby shampoo
5ml (1 tsp) powdered gelatine
few drops essential oil for perfume

Beat the ingredients together with an electric whisk and add to hot running water for a froth of bubbles.

BODY MASSAGE

The soothing effect of your bath should be followed up with a relaxing massage using a specially formulated oil or lotion to lubricate and protect your skin. Your skin is warm and supple after a bath and especially receptive to this form of beauty therapy.

Massage is the key to inner tranquillity and good skin and muscle tone. You do not have to be an expert to be able to follow the simple techniques outlined here and the sooner you get into the habit of regular massage, the sooner your body will show the benefits this treatment can bring. Gentle massage stimulates your circulation and promotes a gleaming, soft skin tone. More vigorous treatment exercises and tones your muscles. Both forms of massage are calmative and bring you to complete relaxation. Never rush a massage – enjoy it as you would any luxurious treat.

TECHNIQUES

Stroking:
Using your whole hand, stroke the surface of your skin with a gentle, rhythmic, soothing movement towards your heart. Use this technique all over your body to relax muscles and promote deep relaxation.

Pinching and kneading:
Both these techniques share the same principle – lifting and squeezing of the flesh. Pinching is a small light movement using your thumbs and fingertips; kneading is a larger movement, exerting more pressure on your flesh.

Use pinching on your upper arms, upper abdomen and where your skin is tight. Use kneading on fleshier areas such as your hips, thighs and buttocks.

Pressing and rolling:
Use the thumbs of both hands to "press and roll" your skin against the pressure of your fingers. Your skin is lifted slightly then massaged smoothly down again with this movement. A very good treatment for plump thighs.

Slapping:
This can be slightly painful if you work too enthusiastically. Do not use it on scarred skin or broken veins. It is a fast, bouncy slapping action using your cupped hands in an alternating rhythm. Use it on the areas of your body where your circulation is most sluggish, such as your thighs, hips, buttocks and stomach.

Prime targets
Maximum release of tension comes from the treatment of key areas in very specific ways.

Legs
△ Gently knead and stroke up your calf. Pinch and stroke around your knee and complete the massage with firm stroking movements at the back of your knee. This massage relieves tension in aching leg muscles and tendons. Combine it with the foot massage *(see p87)* for maximum effect.

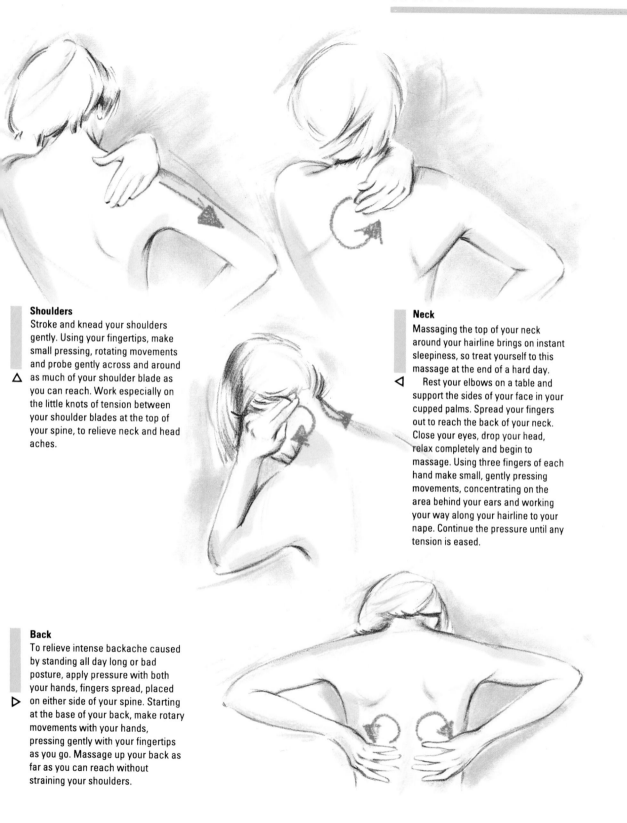

Shoulders
Stroke and knead your shoulders gently. Using your fingertips, make small pressing, rotating movements and probe gently across and around △ as much of your shoulder blade as you can reach. Work especially on the little knots of tension between your shoulder blades at the top of your spine, to relieve neck and head aches.

Neck
Massaging the top of your neck around your hairline brings on instant sleepiness, so treat yourself to this massage at the end of a hard day.
◁ Rest your elbows on a table and support the sides of your face in your cupped palms. Spread your fingers out to reach the back of your neck. Close your eyes, drop your head, relax completely and begin to massage. Using three fingers of each hand make small, gently pressing movements, concentrating on the area behind your ears and working your way along your hairline to your nape. Continue the pressure until any tension is eased.

Back
To relieve intense backache caused by standing all day long or bad posture, apply pressure with both your hands, fingers spread, placed ▷ on either side of your spine. Starting at the base of your back, make rotary movements with your hands, pressing gently with your fingertips as you go. Massage up your back as far as you can reach without straining your shoulders.

BODY CONDITIONING

SIMPLE SECRETS

Body tonic:
Add lemon or lime juice, or witch hazel to the basic rosewater and glycerine moisturizer *(see p36)* to make a good body toning lotion. If you wish, you can substitute elderflower or orange flower water, or an appropriate herbal infusion, for the rosewater in the basic moisturizer recipe.

Body rub:
Keep a large bottle of mixed vegetable oils and add the therapeutic oils of your choice to make a body rub for aching muscles.

Body scrub:
Mix wheat flour or finely ground oatmeal to a paste with double cream and use it as a cleansing softening body scrub.

LANOLIN MASSAGE CREAM

A thick, fairly solid massage cream that ensures an invigorating massage, which improves muscle condition and skin tone.

60ml (4 tbsps) anhydrous lanolin
60ml (4 tbsps) sunflower oil
15ml (1 tbsp) wintergreen camphor or eucalyptus herbal oil (see p21)
195ml (9 tbsps) purified water

Warm the lanolin and the oils together in a bowl in a *bain-marie*. Heat the water to the same temperature in a separate bowl. Beat the water into the lanolin mixture and continue beating until it cools. Spoon into a 275ml (½pt) pot and seal.

APRICOT CREAM

A muscle-toning massage cream with a delicious fragrance. It is ideal for use on areas prone to flabbiness, such as breasts, neck and upper arms.

15ml (1 tbsp) anhydrous lanolin
15ml (1 tbsp) cocoa butter
30ml (2 tbps) apricot oil
15ml (1 tbsp) orange flower water
2.5ml (½ tsp) borax
few drops orange flower (neroli) oil

Melt the lanolin and the cocoa butter together in a bowl in a *bain-marie* and beat in the apricot oil. Warm the orange flower water to the same temperature in a separate bowl and dissolve the borax in it. Beat the water into the oils and continue beating until the mixture is cool. Add the neroli oil. Spoon into a 150ml (¼pt) pot and seal.

VIOLET ESSENCE BODY OIL

A fine thin cream that is easily absorbed.

15ml (1 tbsp) anhydrous lanolin
30ml (2 tbsps) white petroleum jelly
75ml (5 tbsps) baby oil
225ml (⅜pt) purified water
2.5ml (½ tsp) essential oil of violets

Melt the lanolin and oils in a bowl in a *bain-marie*. Heat the water to the same temperature in a separate bowl. Add the water to the lanolin mixture, beating continously. Remove from the heat and beat until cool. Add the violet oil, stir well and spoon into a 275ml (½pt) pot.

ALL-PURPOSE AFTER BATH OIL

A basic everyday massage oil.

60ml (4 tbsps) almond oil
30ml (2 tbsps) wheatgerm oil
45ml (3 tbsps) sunflower oil
45ml (3 tbsps) olive oil
30ml (2 tbsps) sesame oil
15ml (1 tbsp) apricot or avocado oil.
few drops perfume

Shake all the ingredients in a 275ml (½pt) bottle together. Use the perfume of your choice, or keep the oil fragrance-free and add a drop of perfume to a little of the oil when you feel like a change.

SPICY BODY TONER

A fresh tingling body lotion that is ideal for use after an invigorating massage.

15ml (1 tbsp) fresh rosemary
15ml (1 tbsp) fresh mint
pinch fresh grated orange peel
pinch fresh grated lemon peel
pinch grated nutmeg
75ml (5 tbsps) rose or orange flower water
30ml (2 tbsps) alcohol

Blend all the ingredients in a liquidizer. Pour into a glass jar, seal and leave to soften on a warm windowsill for at least a week. Strain and pour into a 150ml (¼pt) bottle.

AVOCADO AND WHEATGERM MASSAGE OIL

A ideal oil to use on sun and sea soaked bodies; it is particularly relaxing after exercise. Almond oil can be substituted for the avocado oil.

60ml (4 tbsps) avocado oil
60ml (4 tbsps) wheatgerm oil

Shake the oils together in a 150ml (¼pt) bottle.

LAVENDER BODY LOTION

A soothing, healing lotion, perfect for a massage last thing at night.

60ml (4 tbsps) almond oil
150ml (¼pt) rosewater
5ml (1 tsp) borax
several drops lavender oil

Warm the almond oil and the rosewater in separate bowls in a *bain-marie*. Dissolve the borax in the water and beat this solution slowly into the oil. Continue beating until the mixture combines without separating and add the lavender oil. Pour into a 275ml (½pt) bottle. Shake well before using.

STAY FRESH

Using a gentle deodorant after washing gives you the confidence that your fresh scented body will stay that way all day long.

SIMPLE SECRETS
To sweeten:
An infusion of crysanthemum leaves, sage or cleavers makes an effective deodorant.
Apple cider vinegar also makes a good deodorant when diluted with two parts purified water.

LAVENDER UNDERARM DEODORANT

A fragrant, long lasting deodorant.

3 drops lavender oil
15ml (1 tbsp) sugar
575ml (1 pt) purified water

Shake the ingredients together in a bottle and leave for two weeks. Decant into an atomizer and shake before using.

SUNSHINE SKIN/1

The gleam of a healthy tanned skin is one of the most sought after natural beauty enhancers and many people will go to extraordinary lengths to acquire it. Though there is no doubt that a tanned face and body can look very attractive, it is vitally important to remember that your skin can be severely damaged by overexposure to the sun's penetrating rays. The price you pay for the superficial glamour of brown skin may be higher than you think.

Too much sun and too little protection from it is bad for your skin – not only superficially in terms of surface burning and dehydration, but at a deeper level. The ultraviolet, or tanning, rays that stimulate increased production of the skin's melanin cells so causing a deepening of the skin's colour, also affect cell structure and disturb the collagen and elastin fibres deep in the dermis, often with permanently disruptive results. Skins exposed to high levels of ultraviolet light are coarser in texture and age prematurely as a result of this structural damage. There is also a far higher incidence of skin cancer among people who live in very hot climates, those who sunbathe to an excessive extent, and those who do not take sensible precautions when their skin is exposed to strong sunlight.

The only way to ensure that your skin does not suffer the harmful effects of exposure to ultraviolet light is to avoid baring any part of it to the sunlight. This is, of course, impossible, so steps have to be taken to minimize long-term damage and short-term discomfort through careful protection and skin nourishment.

Every skin type, from darkest to fairest, is sensitive to ultraviolet light; protecting yours efficiently involves examining how it responds to sunlight and how quickly and comfortably it tans. Very fair skin will show increased sensitivity to sunlight and must be protected accordingly. Having darker more resilient skin or one that is used to constant exposure, however, does not mean that it will not burn. You should protect your skin whenever it is exposed to sunlight to minimize the risk of damage, no matter how well established your tan is. Another important thing to remember is that it is not only when lying on a beach or by a pool on holiday that your skin is in danger. If you are living in a hot climate, you will find that your skin will burn whenever you are outside, whether you are gardening, shopping or playing sport.

You can protect your skin in a number of ways. Wearing a hat and loose cotton clothing is a good idea, but remember that sunlight can filter through light translucent materials, so wear a good protective cream as well. All sunscreens are

A healthy golden tan can be yours if you treat the power of the sun with great respect and protect your skin scrupulously from its damaging rays.

SUNSHINE SKIN/2

categorized by Sun Protection Factor (SPF) numbers ranging from 2-15+ – the higher the SPF number, the longer you can stay in the sun without burning. Sunscreens are very effective if they are chosen carefully, used correctly and reapplied frequently during exposure to the sun. The sun is at its strongest between the hours of 11am and 3pm, so try to avoid long exposure at this tome of day. Remember, though, that the reflected light bouncing off water and snow almost doubles the force of ultraviolet rays, so you must ensure that any exposed skin is very carefully protected before going sailing, windsurfing or skiing. If you are very active in the sun or swim between sunbathing sessions, remember to reapply your protective cream regularly because your perspiration and the sea or pool water will gradually wash it off.

If you treat the sun with due respect, then there is no reason why you should not enjoy it safely. Using a good sunscreen, keeping your skin well-moisturized and nourished with natural products and staggering the length of time you spend in the sun should ensure a comfortable and healthy tan.

Every type of skin, from fairest to darkest, will burn when exposed to strong sunlight unless it is efficiently protected. Wearing a hat, a good sunscreen and avoiding the midday sun will minimize the risk of any irreparable damage.

GOLDEN RULES FOR SUN WORSHIPPERS

Keep your skin in good condition all the year round by nourishing and moisturizing regularly. Supple, well-nourished skin is less susceptible to the drying effects of the sun.

Never be mean with your protective lotion or cream – spread it lavishly on your skin.

Avoid prolonged exposure in the middle of the day.

Pay special attention when applying a protective cream to particularly sensitive areas such as breasts, collarbones, shins, hips and buttocks and any part of your skin that is being exposed for the first time. A new style of swimming costume can often reveal a little more flesh than you may previously have been used to.

Do not forget to protect your eyes by wearing good quality sun glasses, and nourish your hair *(see Protein Oil Conditioner p65)*, which can become very dry and brittle as a result of exposure to strong sunlight and sea or salt water.

Drink plenty of fresh water and eat fresh fruits to keep your body's water levels up during the summer months.

Always moisturize your skin thoroughly after a day in the sun.

SUNSHINE SKIN/3

SIMPLE SECRETS

To moisturize:

Sesame and coconut oils make pleasant all-purpose skin lubricants to keep your skin supple. They afford little or no protection from the sun's burning rays, so use them in conjunction with a good sunscreen if you expect to expose your skin to the sun.

For sunburn:

Rose and glycerine moisturizer *(see p36)* is an effective balm to use on hot, dry skin. It does not protect skin against burning.

CUCUMBER SUN LOTION

This is not a protective lotion, but it is ideal to use as a cooling daily moisturizer if you live in a hot climate.

juice of 1 large cucumber
2.5ml (½ tsp) glycerine

Blend the ingredients together and keep the lotion in the refrigerator. Use within three days.

BASIC SUN OIL

A simple moisturizing oil. The perfume in it acts as an insect deterrent as well as for fragrance.

150ml (¼ pt) sesame oil
75ml (5 tbsps) cider vinegar
5ml (1 tsp) iodine
few drops lavender or verbena essential oil

Shake the ingredients together in a 250ml (9fl oz) bottle.

SUNFLOWER AND LEMON OIL

This fresh-scented oil keeps skin well moisturized.

150ml (¼ pt) sunflower oil
45ml (3 tbsps) fresh lemon juice

Shake the ingredients together in a 200ml (7fl oz) bottle, keep refrigerated and use within five days.

TEA TANNING LOTION

Tea is a natural sunscreening agent. This lotion is mildly protective, moisturizing and gives the skin a light colour.

45ml (3 tbsps) cocoa butter
45ml (3 tbsps) coconut oil
45ml (3 tbsps) sesame or olive oil
75ml (5 tbsps) strong Indian tea
few drops lemon grass essential oil

Melt the cocoa butter and the coconut oil in a bowl in a *bain-marie* and add the sesame or olive oil. Remove from the heat and beat in the warm tea. Continue beating until the mixture cools and add the perfumed oil. Bottle in a 300ml (11fl oz) wide-necked container.

HAIR PROTECTOR

A protective, moisturizing conditioner to comb through your hair before a day in the sun. Shampoo it out when you get home.

45ml (3 tbsps) castor oil
15ml (1 tbsp) coconut oil

Melt the two oils together in a bowl in a *bain-marie*. Use while still warm. Use as much of this at a time as you wish – it keeps indefinitely.

N.B. None of these preparations should be relied upon to provide any substantial degree of protection from ultraviolet burning. They are designed purely as enjoyable alternatives to regular moisturizers for your face and body when the weather is hot.

SUNSHINE SKIN/4

SUNBURN ANTIDOTES

There are few things that cause as much misery as an attack of severe sunburn. Protecting your skin thoroughly and avoiding long exposure to the sun should prevent it, but if you do get sunburnt, there are two important remedial steps to take. Firstly, you need to soothe the pain and secondly you must ensure that the damaged skin does not peel or crack. Immediate treatment and staying out of the sun for a day or two after an attack should minimize any serious suffering.

SIMPLE SECRETS

For all-over relief:
Add either 100g (4oz) bicarbonate of soda, 150ml (¼ pint) cider vinegar, or 275ml (½ pint) strong marigold or camomile infusion *(see p20)* to your bath water.

For specific areas:
Gin, cold sage or Indian tea and infusions of nettle, lettuce leaf, camomile or comfrey *(see p20)* applied to burnt areas with a cotton wool pad will bring relief.
Equal parts of baking soda and water, or the pulps of strawberries or cucumber basted on to the burnt areas will bring relief after about half an hour.

To prevent peeling:
Apply Marigold Oil *(see p51)* to heal the affected skin.
Pumpkin oil heals sunburnt skin and is also a wonderful remedy for chapped, sun-dried hands. A mashed strawberry and buttermilk mask is very healing and soothing.

To soothe and cool:
Wash your burnt skin with milk, or a milk and camomile infusion *(see p20)*.

CALAMINE AND GLYCERINE LOTION

Unless the burning is severe, this lotion will prevent peeling as well as soothe sunburnt skin.

75ml (5 tbsps) calamine lotion
90ml (6 tbsps) purified water
10ml (2 tsps) glycerine

Shake the ingredients together in a 250ml (9fl oz) bottle and apply when necessary.

IODINE SUNBURN LOTION

An antiseptic, healing lotion which helps to prevent peeling. A herbal vinegar made with lavender *(see p21)* is ideal to use in this recipe, because lavender has effective healing properties.

90ml (6 tbsps) olive oil
45ml (3 tbsps) herbal or cider vinegar
2.5ml (½ tsp) iodine

Shake the ingredients together in a 150ml (¼pt) bottle and use when necessary.

ELDERFLOWER LOTION

Windburn can be just as painful and damaging as sunburn. This lotion can be used all over your body to soothe both problems. It is especially useful for those who windsurf or sail.

75ml (5 tbsps) elderflower water (see p20)
75ml (5 tbsps) glycerine
45ml (3 tbsps) witch hazel
15ml (1 tbsp) almond oil
15ml (1 tbsp) eau de cologne
2.5ml (½ tsp) borax

Shake all the ingredients together in a 250ml (9fl oz) bottle. Seal tightly and shake before use. Keep refrigerated.

YOGHURT AND ROSEWATER

A cooling, healing and bleaching cream for sunburnt or windburnt skin.

150ml (¼ pt) yoghurt
30ml (2 tbsps) rosewater

Mix the ingredients together and apply to the affected areas. Use for one application. Elderflower water can be substituted for the rosewater if you prefer.

LIP SALVE

A healing lip balm to use on burnt lips. Skiers will find it especially effective.

10ml (2 tsps) beeswax
10ml (2 tsps) coconut oil
5ml (1 tsp) castor oil

Melt the wax and the coconut oil together in a bowl in a *bain-marie*. Add the castor oil and stir well. Remove from the heat and pot in small jars.

Sun babies

It is imperative that your children's skin receives careful attention when it comes to protection from the sun. Much of the damage caused deep in the dermis of skins that have been exposed to strong sunlight begins at an early age and can pass unnoticed until later life, when it manifests itself in prematurely aged, coarsened skin and the formation of benign growths or, at worst, skin cancer.

A child's skin is exceptionally sensitive to ultraviolet light and you should always make sure that you have applied a sunscreen of SPF 15+ before your children go out into the sun. When it is very hot, you should keep them out of the sun between the hours of 10am and 3pm. Dress toddlers sensibly in opaque cotton clothes and make sure they have hats if they are going to be sitting or playing in the sun. Prams and pushchairs should be fitted with parasols so the sun does not shine directly on to your baby's head when you are out for a walk or when he is left in the garden to rest.

Beach babies

On the beach children are especially prone to sunburn because they spend most of their time running in and out of the sea or rolling in the sand as they play – both these activities result in any cream you have applied coming off their skin. Try to reapply sunscreens as often as you can, paying particular attention to the skin on their necks, around their eyes, on the crest of their cheekbones, on their ears, and on their hands and feet. A beach umbrella is a sound investment, especially if the beach you are on affords no shade whatsoever. Young children often seek shaded areas instinctively when they feel hot or uncomfortable in the sun – danger signs that they are likely to get burnt. Bad temper and sunburn can easily be avoided if some shade is provided. In any event, you should not stay on the beach for longer than two hours when your children are very young. The reflected glare from the sand and the water can be very harsh on children's eyes as well as their skin, so long periods in this environment are not a good idea.

Natural soothers

The same soothing after-sun coolers and sunburn antidotes recommended for your use *(see pp110-11)* can be used with confidence on your children's skin. Thorough moisturizing is as important for young skins as it is for older ones, especially when their natural moisture levels have been upset by the heat. The basic moisturizer designed to care for facial skin *(see p36)* makes a good all over replenishing cream for children's over-heated or wind-dried skin.

The health of their children is always a top priority for mothers. Protecting young children's skin from the harmful effects of strong sunlight by using high protection factor creams is essential. The natural moisturizers *(see p36)*, used to replenish facial skin double as soothers for your children when they have been in the sun.

HANDLE WITH CARE/1

Moisturizing is one of the most important steps in your skin care routine at any time, but especially so when your skin is exposed to strong sunlight, cold winds and central heating. You need to replenish the excessive amount of water that your skin loses in these conditions and provide it with some defence against further dehydration by keeping it well nourished.

The plants and fruits which grow in hot climates have amazing healing properties when applied in their raw state to sun damaged and wind dried skin. Paw-paw and pineapple contain enzymes, fatty acids and vitamins that soften and heal dehydrated skin. The flesh of avocados, peaches and apricots will soothe dry skins, while banana pulp softens and nourishes. You can cool and moisturize your skin with the juice of grapes and watermelons, while the juices of lemons, oranges, tomatoes and sweet peppers work as instant skin tonics and brighteners.

Winter skin needs as much care as summer skin, because the drying effects of the sun's heat and light are replaced by those of radiators and fires. The remedies listed for use on sun damaged skin can be as effectively employed to liven up tired skins suffering from mid-winter blues. Concern for the condition of your skin all year round will prepare it for any climatic change and keep it looking good whatever your environment.

Keep your skin feeling and looking good whatever the temperature with the use of natural intensive skin conditioners and replenishing masks.

HANDLE WITH CARE/2

CONDITIONING NIGHT CREAM

A wonderfully emollient and nourishing cream, ideal for use on sun dried skin.

30ml (2 tbsps) cocoa butter
30ml (2 tbsps) emulsifying wax
15ml (1 tbsp) beeswax
60ml (4 tbsps) sesame oil
15ml (1 tbsp) almond oil
few drops geranium essential oil

Melt the cocoa butter and the waxes in a bowl in a *bain-marie* and beat in the oils. Beat the mixture until it cools and add the perfume. Spoon into a 250ml (9fl oz) pot and seal.

NOURISHING NIGHT CREAM

A rich soothing cream, suitable for use on your body as well as your face.

7.5ml (½ tbsp) beeswax
45ml (3 tbsps) coconut oil
30ml (2 tbsps) olive oil
15ml (1 tbsp) sesame oil
60ml (4 tbsps) orange flower water
2.5ml (½ tsp) borax
few drops neroli or bergamot essential oil

Melt the wax and the coconut oil together in a bowl in a *bain-marie*. Heat the orange flower water to the same temperature in a separate bowl and dissolve the borax in it. Beat the olive oil and the sesame oil into the wax mixture and remove it from the heat. Slowly beat in the flower water. Beat the mixture until it cools and add the perfume. Spoon into a 200ml (7fl oz) pot and seal.

AVOCADO FACE MASK

A softening, nourishing treat for dry, sunburnt or wind dried skin.

30ml (2 tbsps) mashed avocado pulp
5ml (1 tsp) fresh lemon juice
5ml (1 tsp) clear honey

Mix all the ingredients together and apply to your face and neck. Leave on for as long as possible and rinse off with tepid water.

FIG AND THYME MASK

A cooling, moisturizing mask to use on overheated skin. It will also soothe chilblains.

4 fresh ripe figs
15ml (1 tbsp) clear honey
5ml (1 tsp) dried thyme

Simmer the figs in a covered pan with the honey and enough water to cover the mixture. When they are softened, mash the fig and honey well with the crushed thyme. When this mixture is smooth and paste-like in texture, apply it to your face and leave for 20 minutes.

GRAPE FACE PACK

A cleansing and revitalizing mask for dry skin. If you have an oily skin, substitute an egg white for the yolk and honey.

100g (4oz) seedless green grapes
5ml (1 tsp) clear honey
1 egg yolk

Mash the grapes, sieve them and mix the pulp with the honey and enough egg yolk to bind the mixture. Paste the mask on to your face and leave for 15 minutes.

PAPAYA (PAW-PAW) MASK

A healing mask that removes dry, flaking skin. It is ideal for oily skin dehydrated by heat or wind.

1 large ripe papaya

Mash the flesh of the papaya and apply it as a mask to your face. Leave it on your skin for 15 minutes.

PEACH OR APRICOT MASK

An excellent moisturizing mask for dry skin damaged by the sun or wind. Banana can be used in the same way to make a nourishing, softening mask.

2 fresh peaches or 4 fresh apricots
15ml (1 tbsp) olive oil

Mash the peeled fruit until the flesh reduces to a smooth pulp. Mix it with the olive oil to make a paste and spread this lavishly on your face. Leave for 15 minutes.

PINEAPPLE MASK

A refreshing and cleansing mask, suitable for overheated, blemished oily skins.

½ fresh pineapple

Extract the juice from the fruit. Soak enough gauze to cover your face in the juice. Apply the gauze to your face, avoiding the skin around your mouth and eyes. Leave for 15 minutes.

BLEACHING MASK

This mask improves the appearance of oily, sallow skins with the fading remains of a suntan.

30ml (2 tbsps) fuller's earth
15ml (1 tbsp) witch hazel
5ml (1 tsp) clear honey
2.5ml (½ tsp) ground cinnamon

Mix the ingredients into a smooth paste and apply to your face and neck. Leave for 20 minutes.
    Fuller's earth mixed to a paste with lemon or lime juice also makes a whitening, tightening mask.

A REJUVENATING FACE MASK

This is a really luxurious mixture of nourishing ingredients. It is especially effective on dry, tired winter skin suffering from the dehydrating effects of central heating and open fires.

15ml (1 tbsp) powdered brewer's yeast
7.5ml (½ tbsp) natural yoghurt
5ml (1 tsp) lemon juice
5ml (1 tsp) orange juice
5ml (1 tsp) carrot juice
10ml (2 tsps) olive oil

Mix all the ingredients together and apply the mixture to your face with a brush. Leave on your skin for at least 15 minutes.

HERBAL FACE WASH

A healing, soothing cleanser for oily skins roughened by cold, salt winds.

150ml (¼ pt) white wine
30ml (2 tbsps) rosemary leaves
15ml (1 tbsp) lemon balm

Simmer all the ingredients together for 10 minutes. Remove from the heat, cover and leave to cool. Strain the liquid and use on a cotton wool pad morning and evening to cleanse your skin.

HEALING FACE PACK

A very soothing mask suitable for oily skins dried and roughened by cold winds.

150ml (¼ pt) natural yoghurt
1 beaten egg white
finely ground oatmeal

Mix the yoghurt and the egg white together with enough oatmeal to make a thick paste. Apply liberally to your face neck and hands. Leave on your skin for 15 minutes.

HONEY AND ROSEWATER LIP SALVE

A healing balm for sore dry lips.

15ml (1 tbsp) clear honey
5ml (1 tsp) rosewater

Melt the honey and stir in the rosewater. Pot and seal.

CHAPTER FIVE

PERFUME

A woman's perfume is a means of silent communication, revealing her femininity, her sense of humour, her passion or her independence, and choosing the scent that you feel communicates the essence of your personality is an important decision. The process of creating perfumes is highly complex and cannot be achieved at home, but you can make heady floral or spicy colognes and cream perfumes using natural flower waters and essential oils.

PLEASURES OF PERFUME

Choosing your own perfume is a very important undertaking. A person's scent can be the most memorable thing about them and acts as a silent expression of their personality. Certain fragrances conjure up images of fresh meadows, others remind us of specific flowers, while some have an almost tangible musky oriental flavour. No single perfume smells the same on everyone, because it combines with our natural skin secretions to form its ultimate fragrance. Beware of buying a perfume just because you loved its scent on someone else – it might smell completely different on you.

It is impossible to create your own perfume at home, because perfume-making is a meticulously exact scientific process, requiring specialized knowledge and equipment. It is, however, possible to make delicately scented flower waters, colognes and fragrant creams using fresh herbs, flowers and essential oils. You can experiment with various combinations of these ingredients to find the particular scent you like and wish to make your own. Once you have made this decision, you will be able to surround yourself with a luxurious range of cosmetics perfumed with your personal fragrance.

A SIMPLE COLOGNE

15ml (1 tbsp) essential flower oil
425ml (¾ pt) pure alcohol
distilled water

Mix the essential oil with a quarter of the alcohol until it is completely dispersed in it. Slowly add the rest of the alcohol, stirring well. Bottle and seal tightly. Do not use a cork to seal the jar, as it will absorb the fragrance from the cologne. Leave the mixture for one month to mature. Dilute it for use with the distilled water – 2.5ml (½ tsp) cologne to 275ml (½pt) of water.

A wonderful rose petal cologne can be made by standing a jar packed with red rose petals that have been soaked in alcohol on a sunny windowsill for several months. You can soak the petals in white wine vinegar, but the resulting cologne is rather strong and is therefore more suitable for perfuming your bath water than for using directly on your skin.

AN EXOTIC COLOGNE

10 drops essential oil of cloves
20 drops tincture of musk
3 drops essential oil of lavender
575ml (1 pt) pure alcohol
distilled water

Put the oils and the tincture of musk together in a glass
jar and slowly add the alcohol, stirring continuously.
Seal the jar with a plastic lid, shake it well and leave for
one month in a warm place before using. Dilute with the
water using the same proportions as for the Simple
Cologne.

BIGARADE COLOGNE

A very luxurious cologne. Balsam of Peru *(see below)* is
a fixative that comes from the Peruvian Balsam Tree.

7ml (1½ tsps) essential oils of bergamot, neroli, thyme
*   and cloves*
7ml (1½ tsps) Balsam of Peru
150ml (¼ pt) orange flower water
1l (1¾ pts) pure alcohol
distilled water

Put all the ingredients except the alcohol into a glass
jar. Add the alcohol very slowly, stirring constantly with
a plastic spatula. Seal tightly the jar tightly with a plastic
or plastic-lined lid. Leave for at least a month to mature.

BASIC CREAM PERFUME

Cream perfumes last longer because the warmth of your
body gradually causes the scent to diffuse from the film
of cream on your skin.

50g (2oz) grated beeswax
75ml (5 tbsps) almond oil
60ml (4 tbsps) distilled water
20 drops flower cologne
of your choice

Melt the wax in a bowl in a *bain-marie* and slowly beat
in the almond oil. Warm the water to the same
temperature in a separate bowl. Remove both bowls
from the heat and whisk the water into the wax and oil
mixture, followed by the cologne. Beat until the mixture
cools. Spoon into a 850ml (1½pt) pot and seal.

HUNGARY WATER

Substitute your own selection of fragrant flowers, herbs
or leaves with added spices such as nutmeg, cinnamon
and coriander for those suggested here.

60ml (4 tbsps) fresh chopped mint
60ml (4 tbsps) shredded red rose petals
45ml (3 tbsps) fresh crushed rosemary
15ml (1 tbsp) freshly grated orange peel
15ml (1 tbsp) freshly grated lemon peel
1.25ml (¼ tsp) ground cloves
150ml (¼ pt) orange flower water
150ml (¼ pt) pure alcohol

Pound the dry ingredients in a mortar with a pestle and
put them in a large glass jar. Add the orange flower
water, followed by the alcohol, stirring constantly to
ensure the mixture is well combined. Seal the jar with a
plastic lid and leave to macerate for two weeks on a
warm windowsill. Strain through a filter paper into a
400ml (14fl oz) bottle and seal.
Leave for a further two weeks
before using.

ESSENTIAL OILS

The process of extracting the precious volatile oils from plants and flowers is highly complicated and costly and cannot be undertaken at home. All good herbalists stock a wide range of essential oils, so there should be no problem obtaining them for use in cosmetic recipes.

Other special oils used in this book are pharmaceutical and herbal oils. Pharmaceutical oils are available from good chemists and include wintergreen and camphor oils. Eucalyptus and peppermint oils are also available in this form. They are used in body rubs and in some cosmetics. They are less refined than essential oils and are economical to use over large areas of the body. Herbal oils are made by steeping herbs in vegetable oil *(see p21)*. They are not as concentrated as essential oils and cannot be substituted for them in recipes.

Angelica:	A sweet and musky oil used in skin tonics and to perfume the bath.
Bay:	A pungent oil used in colognes, bath oils and invigorating massage oils.
Benzoin:	A vanilla scented fixative oil used in cosmetics and massage oils.
Bergamot:	A spicy citrus oil used in tanning lotions and moisturizing creams for oily skins.
Camomile:	A light, floral oil used in creams and lotions for dry skins and for its soothing and healing properties in bath oils.
Cedarwood:	A woody oil used to treat skin and hair disorders.
Cinnamon:	A warm, spicy oil used to perfume the bath.
Clove:	A pungent, spicy oil used in the bath and in massage oils for its antiseptic and mild pain-killing properties.
Cypress:	A green, aromatic oil used in the bath and massage oils to aid circulatory problems.

Eucalyptus:	An aromatic, pungent oil used in the bath, in massage oils and in saunas for its antiseptic and invigorating properties.
Geranium:	A floral, conditioning oil used in cosmetics for ageing skins and for its healing and soothing properties in the bath and in massage creams.
Jasmin:	A sweet, floral oil used in cosmetics and as a calmative in the bath.
Juniper:	A green, pungent oil used in cosmetics to cure skin irritations and in the bath to promote sleep.
Lavender:	A strongly aromatic, healing and antiseptic oil used in cosmetics and in soothing bath and massage oils.
Lemon grass:	A sweet, lemon-scented, antiseptic and deodorizing oil used in baths and massage oils.
Lemon verbena:	A sharp, lemon-scented oil used in cosmetics for oily skins and in the bath to refresh.
Marigold:	A green, fragrant oil with healing and rejuvenating properties, used in cosmetics, in the bath and in massage oils to soothe strains.
Orange blossom or neroli:	A floral, orange-scented oil used in healing and rejuvenating cosmetics, and in the bath and massage oils to calm and soothe.
Patchouli:	A sweet, spicy antiseptic oil used in cosmetics for oily skins, shampoos and bath oils.
Peppermint:	A minty, stimulating oil used in skin tonics, in the bath and as an antiseptic in mouth washes.
Pine:	A balsamic oil which has refreshing, soothing and revitalizing effects in the bath.